Is God A Capitalist?

God's Perspective On Governments and Economic Systems

Gregory B Grinstead

Copyright

Is God A Capitalist?

God's Perspective On Governments and Economic Systems
Copyright by Gregory B Grinstead

Second Printing February 2016

Books > Christian > Politics
Books > Christian > Conservative Values
Books > Conservative > Politics

ISBN-13: 978-1530156078

ISBN-10: 1530156076

Contents

CONTENTS

Dedication

This book is dedicated to

My wife Michelle

You are my gift from God

Your love gives me confidence to do new things

A Note to the Reader

I am writing this book to Christians and those who believe in the God who created the universe.

Does the Bible give us clear information about what God thinks? This may seem like a stupid question, until you start to listen to the many different opinions Christians have about politics, governments and financial systems. As you read this book, you will find that atheists over the last two centuries have been unified in their beliefs. They do not like Capitalists or Free Markets.

But we Christians, who should have greater insight and a clearer understanding about men's affairs, do not have a consistent, Bible based view of governments. Intersecting with this confusion about governments is the responsibility of American Christians to "self-rule." Too many leaders in the Body of Christ have given the responsibility to teach about this subject to Fox News and MSNBC.

When it comes to God's thoughts and commands about how to treat their neighbor in a micro (one on one) situation, most Christians agree. But when it comes to the two ingredients that are essential to be good citizens, Christian leaders leave these concepts to unbeliever's opinions and personal preferences. To succeed in making a nation with Bible based values, Christians must:

1. Be involved in politics
2. Have a Bible based value system that guides their politics

Does the Bible clearly tell us God's thoughts on these matters?

Let us explore what the Bible says.

Introduction

Sunday morning should be a politics free zone.

Those who attend church should have an uplifting spiritual time away from the confusion of politics, economic worries and the darkness of our world.

I was senior pastor of a Southern California church for over 25 years and approached Sunday as a time of rest, inspiration and instruction about spiritual matters, not Fox News and the issues of the day.

But by ONLY teaching the most important things, like loving God and loving others, we church leaders have left the church ignorant on what God says about politics, governments and economic systems.

Is Politics Bad?

"I don't like politics." You can hear it at every church, no matter the denomination. "That's just politics." Or "That guy is just playing politics."

Charles Krauthammer's introduction of his best-selling book *Things That Matter* stated the need for good men to participate in politics.

> While science, medicine, art, poetry, architecture, chess, space, sports, number theory and all things hard and beautiful promise purity, elegance and sometimes even transcendence, they are fundamentally subordinate. In the end they must bow to the sovereignty of politics.

> Politics, the crooked timber of our communal lives, dominates everything because, in the end, everything – high and low and, most especially, high – lives or dies by politics. You can have the most advanced and efflorescent of cultures. Get your politics wrong, however, and everything stands to be swept away. This is not ancient history. It is Germany 1933 [1]

---

[1] Things That Matter by Charles Krauthammer; Crown Forum

Is God A Capitalist?

Politics is about how we corporately treat one another. Secular politics is about how we express love outside the church. Politics is about how we communicate our differences with one another, in the issues we feel are the most important. Politics is more than personal preference. Many times it encompasses moral issues that good men must discuss.

Does God have a strong opinion on how men relate to one another? Our lives unfold slowly and we process our lives through the events in real time. As we mature, learn and walk with God, we should grow more clear on what God prefers; what God prefers in secular politics.

The title of this book is partially tongue and cheek. But in the light of God having a preference in how men treat one another, we should know the answer to this book's subtitle. What are God's preferences when it comes to Governments and Economic Systems?

Christian Evangelicals have two social issues that they feel, "Are moral and not political." This phrase is used regularly by my fellow pastors. "This is a moral issue, not a political issue." I would suggest there are more than two issues that are both political and moral issues.

In the United States we have the responsibility of self-rule. Christians should be a part of this process. And Christians should bring their uniquely Christian and moral perspective to this process. We should stop acting, as if it is OK to avoid all issues but the "moral issues."

I expect the anti-religion crowd to bully religious people into silence. But if there is one place the morals of religion are needed it is regarding the laws that our government enacts to control our free markets.

"God Said It and That Settles It"

We Christians have one danger when approaching secular politics with a Christian perspective. We should never bring God into an argument and expect the other side to accept our morals. But once the Bible has given us God's wisdom, we can bring that wisdom into the public discourse, without playing the God card.

The others in the public square have their gods too. They do not recognize the authority of the Bible. Others take twisted Bible doctrines as a confirmation to what their atheist college professor taught them. Either way taking the approach in politics that, "God said it and that settles it," is a losing position.

Once you are clear about what the Bible says is a moral government and moral financial system, you can make a moral argument that has history and common sense on our side.

Pastoral Confusion Births Christian Confusion

Some Christian pastors have a lot in common with Socialists. Pastors, educators and bureaucrats all exist in a Zero Sum economic system. The church takes in $10 and spends $10 and the $10 is gone. This is a Zero Sum economic system. Colleges take in $10 and spend $10 and it is gone. Democratic Socialists take in $10…

When you hear your elected official, college professor or your pastor say, "The rich get richer, and the poor get poorer," they are quoting the reality of a person who functions in a Zero Sum Economy. This falsehood makes a lot of sense to them. It is their financial reality.

The rest of us live and work in a different world. We view work as a time of creating value and getting paid for the value we create. For-profit businesses take in one dollar and spend the dollar as they make three more. If the For-profit business does not do this, it quickly stops existing as a business.

As you read on you will discover that this economic illiteracy is allowing many atheist's views to be repeated, with great conviction, from our pulpits. Karl Marx, viewed religion as *the opium of the masses* and religion is used by the rich ruling class to give false hope to the poor. He called this the *Law of Increasing Poverty.*

Next Sunday morning the zealous young, college educated leader at your church will never say, "Now I am going to quote Karl Marx."

This young man may think that the Bible really doesn't address the complicated issues of our times. Or his thinking may be infected by the arrogance of the well-educated. It is a real asset to be well-educated when using that education in the physical sciences. It is a great disadvantage if you have been well-educated by today's social science educators.

I would ask you to become teachable in these areas, where everyone ALREADY has an opinion – sometimes a strong opinion. Strong opinions isolate us from new thinking and make us unteachable. Let us explore the Bible's ideas about free markets, governments and how they affect our country, with a teachable mind.

Does God have an opinion about all this?

Read on.

1

Adam Had a Job in the Garden
The Ennobling Power of Work

The LORD God took the man and placed him in
The Garden of Eden to work it and watch over it.
Genesis 2:15 HCSB

The approach we take to work becomes a part of the foundation of economics systems. A nation's perspective on work defines its values. For most of human history work was mandatory. If you didn't produce something, you did not eat. As the Industrial Revolution progressed the connection between work and food was blurred. Then with the success of the Free Markets and the riches that came with hard work, the connection was broken. Now there are many people confused about why we need to work. As anti-capitalists search for their Garden of Eden, they have forgotten that Adam had a job in the Garden.

Man Was Created for Relationship
Man Was Created to Work

These two purposes of God for man started before Adam's sin. These two purposes precede the futility that creation was subjected to, as Adam was forced from the Garden of Eden.

We will probably never know Adam's full job description in the Garden. We know it was not a time of futility or confusion, so I assume Adam got up every day with the joyful realization that he had another day to walk with God and work in the Garden.

But what does this have to do with us. We live in the age of futility described in Genesis 3:17-18 and Romans 8:20-21.

And He *(God)* said to Adam, "Because you listened to your wife's voice and ate from the tree about which I commanded you, 'Do not eat from it':

> The ground is cursed because of you.
> You will eat from it by means of painful labor
> all the days of your life.
> It will produce thorns and thistles for you,
> and you will eat the plants of the field.
> *Genesis 3:17-18 HCSB*

For the creation was subjected to futility—not willingly, but because of Him who subjected it—in the hope that the creation itself will also be set free from the bondage of corruption into the glorious freedom of God's children. *Romans 8:20-21 HCSB*

God's Wisdom - Subjecting Creation to Futility

If God has cursed the ground so that it is harder to get a positive outcome from our work, shouldn't we avoid the pain of work, all together? Should we work hard, if God has cursed our work life? Shouldn't we just focus on our relationships and not worry about what we will accomplish in this life?

In the above "curse of the ground" God is not saying that work is bad and we should avoid it. Nor is He saying that we should measure the success of our lives in how many vacation days we have each year.

God is stating (you could say commanding) a change in our work environment. Adam was created to love God and work in the Garden. As Adam fulfilled these two purposes of life, he enjoyed the experience. Love and work were not disconnected. You probably would have loved your job in the Garden too. The Garden of Eden had no tardiness problems and no termination policies.

The "curse of the ground" changed Adam's job environment. Instead of being free to create, manage and administrate with a 100% production rate, it would be much harder to get things accomplished. The environment Adam lived in would not help him produce.

This was the most loving thing God could do for Adam and the rest of the human race. If fallen men had continued in a Garden of Eden "super-productive" work life with a sinful heart, evil would have increased exponentially. Even with the curse upon creation, human accomplishments quickly increased. As we read the early chapters of Genesis, we see God's sadness in what man had so quickly become. From the stories of Nimrod, Babel and finally Noah, God's love for mankind turns to a deep loving grief.

> Then the LORD saw that the wickedness of man was great on the earth, and that every intent of the thoughts of his heart was only evil continually. The LORD was sorry that He had made man on the earth, and He was grieved in His heart.
>
> The LORD said, "I will blot out man whom I have created from the face of the land, from man to animals to creeping things and to birds of the sky; for I am sorry that I have made them." But Noah found favor in the eyes of the LORD. *Genesis 6:5-8 NASB*

These men, whom God had created with such potential to create and build, had turned their ability to accomplish great things into accomplishing great evil. What would have happened to the Earth, if God in His love, had not subjected the Earth to futility?

The Attack on the Work Ethic

Since the connection between eating and working has been broken in the Western culture, new anti-work doctrines have brought more confusion to our world. Anti-capitalists trying to re-create a Utopia, or secular Garden of Eden, have created Systems that value the time NOT working instead of the time working. Days off, three or four day weekends and more vacation days have replaced the work ethic.

Trying to teach the right balance, priority and perspective many pastors teach a hidden anti-work doctrine and call it Christian. We have all heard the universally accepted truth about the man on his death bed. If you haven't, it goes something like this.

A man on his death bed never regrets spending less time at work. This simplistic anti-work doctrine is never challenged as a post-Industrial Age concept, propagated by men who have always had enough to eat. It also does not take into account the centuries of men who worked painfully hard for their families, BECAUSE they loved them and because they had to support them.

Obviously there are times when men neglect their families by not having a Bible based Work Ethic. Non-Bible based work produces men who are slaves to their work. God has addressed this problem in one of His Ten Morality Pronouncements. There is no need to develop an eleventh Commandment. "Thou Shalt Not Work Too Hard."

Many Christian men, at the end of their lives will have deep regrets that they did not accomplish the things God had for them to accomplish with their skills and talents. Christian men on their death beds will regret being deceived and not working harder for those that they loved. Pastors should reinforce a Bible based work ethic.

Our culture has substituted the bumper sticker - *I am spending my kid's inheritance* - for Proverbs 13:22.

> A good man leaves an inheritance
> to his children's children...
> *Proverbs 13:22 NASB*

Our Christian culture has fallen into agreement, at times with the Socialist's doctrines on work. We now condemn the man who works hard as a workaholic. Christians exhort men and women to spend more time with their family and stop working so hard.

Mandated Rest with a Heart to Work

"Remember the sabbath day, to keep it holy. Six days you shall labor and do all your work, but the seventh day is a sabbath of the Lord your God; in it you shall not do any work, you or your son or your daughter, your male or your female servant or your cattle or your sojourner who stays with you. For in six days the Lord made the heavens and the earth, the sea and all that is in them, and rested on the seventh day; therefore the Lord blessed the Sabbath day and made it holy. *Exodus 20:8-11 NASB*

Adam Had a Job in the Garden

Exodus 20:8-11 reveals God's heart for work. The Creator of Heaven and Earth worked 6 days and then rested one day. God does not want us to be slaves to our work. Therefore He has mandated a day off every six days. One day of rest and contemplation of spiritual matters and six days of creating, producing and serving in the physical world.

6 - Work Days in a week
7 - Prayer Times in a week
1 - Day off in a week
2 - Weeks of feasts and Sabbath celebrations- plus

God has given each of His children three regularly scheduled appointments; daily prayer times, weekly Sabbaths and annual feast times. God established a balance between work and rest times in a culture that did not take time off the job, in harvest times. As a boy in Iowa in the 1950's, my friends would be excused from school to help the family bring in the crops, especially if it was a dry time in a rainy year. God required His children to rest even if it wasn't convenient.

How Can Old People Work?

Capitalism is viewed as heartless, when we talk about the work ethic. When we talk about rewarding the worker, by letting the markets set the wages that they are worthy to receive, opponents say, "So you want the 60 year old guy working digging ditches?"

Bible based Capitalism has fewer old people in poverty than in any other system. There are many reasons, such as honoring the aged and families taking care of their elderly. But the obvious reason is sometimes overlooked.

Free markets and capitalism have more opportunities to find a job that a person can excel at. By trying different jobs, the individual can find the job they are good at. Two things then happen. First – they are happy in their work. Almost everyone likes working in the job that they are good at. Since few are good at what they do at first, they have to stick with it for a while or try other jobs.

The Second thing that happens when they find a job that they are good at is that they have the opportunity to master their job. The older you get the better you get. The people who find where their skill set intersects with production become masters of their jobs. These masters are usually promoted from the physical laborers and they are worth their weight in gold.

These masters of their jobs are all around us; older senior managers who can make accurate and quick decisions; older client managers who serve their clients with joy; older office managers that can organize and develop the processes that remove confusion and make everyone's lives easier. These masters at their jobs are only found in free markets.

Free markets allow older people to set their priorities differently. Because free markets increase everyone's opportunity, senior citizens may pick something new as they get older. They are much more qualified to make these decisions on a personal level than a government regulator. Whether it is early retirement or a late life career change, people have more options.

The answer is "No, 60 year olds won't be digging ditches." And the freer the job markets are, the more likely the aged will feel like valued members of the culture as they follow their own paths.

The Sluggard and the Ant
The Blessing of Knowing Your Degree of Laziness

The Christian work ethic should be modeled by Christians. Much of the world would like to come to America to WORK. They are looking for the opportunities to accomplish more; the freedom to build a future for their kids; the security of a stable work environment. Why? Because Americans have modeled hard work, and have allowed free markets to fairly reward those who are productive and punish the lazy.

If a nation maintains the freedom to work and lets free markets set worker wages, those who do not work will hopefully regain a lost concept. Work is connected to eating. From there they will be motivated to accomplish something with the precious hours of their lives. They may choose to do something with their lives and fight their natural tendencies to be lazy.

Adam Had a Job in the Garden

Christians should never be deceived by the doctrines of big government. They say, "All men will work if the government just gives them a job or creates more jobs." Many secularists become offended when we have the audacity to suggest that men are lazy and don't like to work. At the same time, the secularist puts more value on his own hours away from work, proving the Christian's position, that given the choice, humans prefer leisure time to work time.

I gave my kids chores, all through their childhood. Not because I needed the work done. It would have been easier, many times to do it myself. My intention was to teach them the value of work.

I would say, "Do this for one hour and you get $3.50." Work is sometimes really hard and there will be many times that you will not want to work. By confronting this basic anti-work attitude in their childhood, I am pleased to say that my kids work hard as adults. All four of my children earned money to buy their first cars. This sense of accomplishment can only be experienced by those who work.

> The desire of the sluggard puts him to death,
> For his hands refuse to work;
> All day long he is craving,
> While the righteous gives and does not hold back
> *Proverbs 21:25-26 NASB*

> Go to the ant, O sluggard,
> Observe her ways and be wise,
> Which, having no chief, Officer or ruler,
> Prepares her food in the summer
> *And* gathers her provision in the harvest.
> How long will you lie down, O sluggard?
> When will you arise from your sleep?
> "A little sleep, a little slumber,
> A little folding of the hands to rest"—
> Your poverty will come in like a vagabond
> And your need like an armed man.
> *Proverbs 6:6-11 NASB*

The Christian Path to success;
  1. Fight your nature to avoid hard work
  2. Work hard at whatever job you have at the time
  3. Try different things and discover what you are good at
  4. Seek God's help in finding and doing your work
  5. Once you find something that you are good at - work harder
  6. Master as many things as you can – by setting goals
  7. Whatever you do and whatever your position, serve others
  8. Be faithful to complete your commitments

Each day, I get up and ask God, "What do I have to do today?"
"What can I do today?"
"God, what do you have for me to do today?"

Life is full of thousands of opportunities. We are only limited by the length of each day and the level of our energy. Life is full of doing new things and mundane things. It is full of WORK.

Don't miss out on your next opportunity to succeed.
  Accomplish something in the realm of the creative;
  Accomplish something in the area of the mundane;
  Accomplish something in spiritual realms;
  Produce something of value in the physical world;
  WORK.

2

God's View of Property Ownership

One of my wife's favorite things is to sit on the southwest coast of Maui and look out at the ocean. There are three islands visible from the beaches of Southwest Maui and Lanai is the largest.

In June 2012, as the sun was setting behind the Island of Lanai, the news broke that Lawrence J. Ellison, chief executive of Oracle had bought 98 % of the 141 square mile island from Castle & Cooke.

My wife, looked at me and said, "How can someone buy an Hawaiian Island? Is that legal?" I suppose a large percentage of Americans probably would react in a similar way. "How can one man buy one of the Hawaiian Islands?"

Is It Legal to Own an Hawaiian Island?

The answer, of course is, "Why wouldn't it be?" Private ownership of land is what has made the United States a great country, not government ownership of land. Public ownership is when no one owns the land. Ownership by definition requires ownership rights. The government enforces all ownership rights on all government land. It restricts the public's access and use. The public do not have any rights associated with government land. So why is it called public lands?

The Federal Government owns a tiny percentage of the 13 original states. But it owns approximately 58% of 10 of the Western States. Because the government owns such vast holdings in states like Nevada (84.5%) and Utah (57.4%) its total land ownership is over one quarter of the land mass of the country.[2] It is the large land holdings of the government that now confuses so many of us. We should own more land and the government should own less.

---

[2] http://bigthink.com/strange-maps/291-federal-lands-in-the-us

Commandment 8
You shall not steal.
(Exodus 20:15)

Commandment 10
You shall not covet your neighbor's house;
You shall not covet your neighbor's wife
Or his male servant or his female servant
Or his ox or his donkey
Or anything that belongs to your neighbor.
(Exodus 20:17)

God makes Ten Statements about what is right and what is wrong. These Ten Commandments set the foundation of Christian morality. Two of the ten are directly related in how we view and treat other people's stuff. Whatever you believe about historical injustices or colonialism, God's view of righteous financial dealings between humans includes property ownership.

There are many property laws in the full Law of Moses. This set of laws, helped a group of ex-slaves become a nation within a few generations. Western Civilization has defined contract law and defined property law but God defined it first. One can disagree about the application of these laws. But one cannot disagree that God has an opinion about property ownership. He was very precise when establishing property ownership in the Law of Moses.

The Law of Moses' Property Rights
"If someone sells a home in a walled city, for a full year after it is sold, the person has the right to buy it back. But if the owner does not buy back the house before a full year is over, it will belong to the one who bought it and to his future sons. The house will not go back to the first owner at Jubilee. But houses in small towns without walls are like open country; they can be bought back, and they must be returned to their first owner at Jubilee."

"The Levites may always buy back their houses in the cities that belong to them. If someone buys a house from a Levite, that house in the Levites' city will again belong to the Levites in the Jubilee. This is because houses in Levite cities belong to the people of Levi; the Israelites gave these cities to them. Also the fields and pastures around the Levites' cities cannot be sold, because those fields belong to the Levites forever. *Leviticus 25:29-32 NCV*

Lease Hold or Fee-Simple

Because of God's special covenant with Abraham, the lease hold ownership of land assured the land reverted back to the original designated owner's family in the Year of Jubilee. They can buy the land and own the land with all private ownership rights, with the condition that in a designated year the land and the improvements on it will revert back to a designated owner. The special conditions and protection of the Levite's property ownership was stricter, due to the nature of the Levite's mission to the nation.

Fee-simple land sales give full ownership rights to the buyer forever. In the scripture above all land sold within a walled city was sold as fee-simple unless it was a Levite's house or land.

Non-Biblical Property Ownership

1. I own the land until someone bigger takes it from me.
2. Mother Earth owns the land but the strong get ownership rights.
3. The government owns the land and no one gets ownership rights.
4. The community owns the land and no one gets ownership rights, unless the powerful gives ownership rights to them, temporarily.

Which option protects the individual who has invested time, money and sweat into building something for his family? Land and other property ownership laws instituted and protected by a stable government allow all men to live peacefully together. It enables civilization. Property ownership encourages good stewardship. The natural consequences of bad property stewardship discourage men from being lazy or irresponsible.

Is God A Capitalist?

Jesus Was Not a Socialist
New Testament Confirmations of Property Rights

Then Jesus began teaching them with stories: "A man planted a vineyard. ... Then he leased the vineyard to tenant farmers and moved to another country.

At the time of the grape harvest, he sent one of his servants to collect his share of the crop. But the farmers grabbed the servant, beat him up, and sent him back empty-handed. The owner then sent another servant, but they insulted him and beat him over the head. The next servant he sent was killed. Others he sent were either beaten or killed, until there was only one left—his son whom he loved dearly.

The owner finally sent him, thinking, 'Surely they will respect my son.' "But the tenant farmers said to one another, 'Here comes the heir to this estate. Let's kill him and get the estate for ourselves!' So they grabbed him and murdered him and threw his body out of the vineyard.

"What do you suppose the owner of the vineyard will do?" Jesus asked. "I'll tell you—he will come and kill those farmers and lease the vineyard to others. Didn't you ever read this in the Scriptures?

> 'The stone that the builders rejected
> has now become the cornerstone.
> This is the LORD's doing,
> and it is wonderful to see.'"

The religious leaders wanted to arrest Jesus because they realized he was telling the story against them—they were the wicked farmers. *Mark 12:1-12 NLV*

Jesus in this story equates God as the owner of a vineyard leasing to farmers. He clearly states that the "poor farmers" were the bad guys of the story.

I can image how a socialist Jesus' story might have been just a little bit different. I am assuming that the socialist, communist or Mother Earth Jesus would have not equated a good God to a – horror of horrors – vineyard owner. And then saying he was leasing and sharing in the profit of the land – double gasp.

Socialist Jesus would picture the vineyard owner as the bad guy; the leasing farmers as the helpless victims; and the murdered servants as, "Getting what they deserved." They were oppressing the poor and exploiting the helpless. But there was no Socialist Jesus. He does not exist in any Biblical accounts.

Was the First Century Church Socialist?

There is only one scripture passage that at first glance seems to suggest that the early church was living in a utopian socialist state. But a closer look at the passage confirms Old Testament private ownership laws and the personal responsibility that goes with it.

> And the congregation of those who believed were of one heart and soul; and not one *of them* claimed that anything belonging to him was his own, but all things were common property to them....
>
> For there was not a needy person among them, for all who were owners of land or houses would sell them and bring the proceeds of the sales and lay them at the apostles' feet, and they would be distributed to each as any had need. *Acts 4:32, 35 NASB*

Acts 4 and 5 continues with the story about Barnabas selling a tract of land and giving the money to the Apostles. Then Ananias and Sapphira also sold a piece of land and publically made it a gift to the Apostles, but with wrong intentions. They had kept back a portion of the money. The Apostle Peter's statement to them actually confirms the Early Church's doctrinal position on personal property ownership.

> Peter said, "Ananias, why has Satan filled your heart to lie to the Holy Spirit and to keep back *some* of the price of the land? While it remained *unsold*, did it not remain your own?

And after it was sold, was it not under your control? Why is it that you have conceived this deed in your heart? *Acts 5:3-4 NASB*

Peter's comments are not the comments of someone leading a commune, where everyone is strongly encouraged to support the community. He specifically states that Ananias' property was owned by Ananias and the proceeds of the property were his to do with as he wished. Instead of the abolishing of personal property rights, for good of the whole community, the accounts show the confirming of property rights.

The confusion about the First Century Church is rooted in a misunderstanding of the generous givers of the stories of Acts 4 and 5. Sincere Christians put less importance on how much is in their bank account. Their generous giving quickly developed into a problem of administration of the items being given to the church.

The apostles did not want to be bogged down, by the administration of these gifts and delegated the distribution of the gifts, to faithful (trustworthy) members of the congregation. The Apostles, after stating the qualifications of these ministries, let the congregation choose the men who would steward the gifts; probably one of the first church elections. *Acts 6:1-6*

This story is not a story of socialism but the recounting of a very fluid situation that lasted a short time in church history. The stories actually show that the church quickly de-centralized; delegated authority; instituted a vote to pick the servants that would distribute the charity of the rich.

This scenario is still working today. Faithful men, well known to the congregation are given authority to serve and administrate funds for the church's missions; local and foreign. Generous gifts are given voluntarily to help those in need.

3

God Tells Us His Choice of Governments

Limited with Ten Commandment Values

Ask anyone, "What is the best form of government?" If the person is an American, there is only one answer. Of course, Democracy is the only good form of government. Then they will compare the United States' Democracy to some other form of totalitarian or oppressive government. They may even quote Winston Churchill. "Democracy is the worst form of government, except for all those other forms that have been tried from time to time." *(House of Commons speech, Nov. 11, 1947)*[3]

Today's opinion, that Democracy is the best form of government has not always been held. Aristotle wrote in *The Politics* that he divided governments into 6 types, three good and three bad. He categorized governments by their motives toward those they ruled. [4]

GOOD
King - One man ruling with only good for all.
BAD
Tyranny - One man ruling with selfish intentions.
GOOD
Aristocracy - A group of men rule for the common good.
BAD
Oligarchy - A group of men rule with selfish intent.
GOOD
Polity (Republic) - The majority rule for the common good.
BAD
Democracy - The majority rule with self centered intentions.

---

[3] ais.stanford.edu/Democracy/democracy_DemocracyAndChurchill(090503).html
[4] Wiker, Benjamin (2010-05-25). 10 Books Every Conservative Must Read: Plus Four Not to Miss and One Impostor (Ch. 1). Regnery Publishing. Kindle Edition.

This distinction between the republic and democracy is not just semantics. It is important for Christians to understand. An uninvolved electorate that only votes for its self-interests is a bad form of government. The United States Constitution's Bill of Rights was included because the founders were very concerned with what they called "The Tyranny of the Majority."

The Founding Fathers of the United States tried to avoid the "Rule of the Masses," by creating several safeguards. These included;

The Division of Powers,
The Supermajority,
Strong State Governments,
Limited Federal Powers,
The Electoral College

You might recognize some of the above safeguards that the founders built into our government systems to avoid the Tyranny of the Majority. Can you name the ones that are presently under attack? Or more important, do you know what these safeguards are and how they stop BAD Democracy? Sadly, all these safeguards are being eroded and we now have an ever increasing oppressive government system, our self-seeking democracy.

God Tells Samuel His View of Government

Now Samuel judged Israel all the days of his life. He used to go annually on circuit to Bethel and Gilgal and Mizpah, and he judged Israel in all these places. *I Samuel 7:15-16 NASB*

Then all the elders of Israel gathered together and came to Samuel at Ramah; and they said to him, "Behold, you have grown old, and your sons do not walk in your ways. Now appoint a king for us to judge us like all the nations."

But the thing was displeasing in the sight of Samuel when they said, "Give us a king to judge us." And Samuel prayed to the LORD. The LORD said to Samuel, "Listen to the voice of the people in regard to all that they say to you, for they have not rejected you, but they have rejected Me from being king over them... Now then, listen to their voice; however, you shall solemnly warn them and tell them of the procedure of the king who will reign over them." *I Samuel 8:4-7, 9 NASB*

The nation of Israel disregarded God's warnings about having a Centralized Federal Monarchy like all the other nations. Their need for a system with enough power to control Samuel's sons made them ask for a more oppressive system. If the nation had a good King, they would still NOT be as free, but could feel secure with a powerful national government. If the nation had a bad king, they would feel the oppression of a tyrant.

God told his naive children that seeking a national monarchy would have a negative impact on their lives. Samuel speaks for God and details the burdens of having a national government. The expense of a standing army; the servicing of government bureaucracies; the higher mandatory taxes; God's warnings to Israel look tame compared to the abuses of central governments of the 20th Century.

Samuel ends God's warnings to the nation with;
Then you will cry out in that day because of your king whom you have chosen for yourselves, but the Lord will not answer you in that day.

... the people refused to listen... and they said, "No, but there shall be a king over us, that we also may be like all the nations, that our king may judge us and go out before us and fight our battles." *I Samuel 8:18-20 NASB*

"Power Corrupts and Absolute Power Corrupts Absolutely"

Through the ages, the above quote of Lord Acton has been confirmed over and over again. As I typed these words, a respected Christian brother sent a Twitter message, *"Power doesn't corrupt; power gives your corruption an opportunity to shine."* We can be as naïve as Israel in Samuel's day. "Power" should be viewed as a corrupting influence on every man. The Christian view of humanity is that ALL humans are flawed. All, good and bad can be corrupted.

The Privileges of Power Corrupt

The last two Judges of Israel had proven this concept. Eli and Samuel's sons were not ready to judge the nation. They had allowed the privileges of power to corrupt them. In the stories told about Eli's sons, it is evident that their father's position gave them special privileges. Positions of power and authority bring benefits that can be used and exploited.

Eli's sons exploited or used these privileges and scared the regional leaders of the nation. The Nation of Israel saw Samuel's sons as unfit to lead. And instead of returning to their communities and maintaining the very limited authority of the national judges, they asked for One Man rule. The human tendency is to look to the next man for salvation. Wait until the next election and someone else will rescue the nation.

That is the confusion of the above tweet. Power isn't corrupting if people are corrupt. Power has the potential of corrupting everyone, no matter how good intentioned the leader.

What Form of Government
Was God Pleased With?

The *Time of the Judges* is viewed by most Christian leaders, as a time of chaos and lawlessness. Pastors have the authority of either the King or Aristocracy. This form of church government keeps things ordered and neat. Even in the best Elderships (Aristocracy) there is a chief elder who rules with the help of the other elders. This mindset may be one reason why many Christian leaders dislike or avoid the obvious truth of *The Times of The Judges*.

God preferred the governmental structure of the *Times of the Judges*. God did not want Israel to have a strong national government. God had guided the nation as they transformed from a large, unruly group of slaves to a nation practicing self-rule; a nation with a set of laws.

God Tells Us His Choice of Government

This freedom established by God allowed the messiness of self-rule that is chronicled in *The Times of the Judges*. It is described accurately by the writers of the Bible with one comment that every pastor has quoted. I feel we may have misquoted it.

> In those days there was no king in Israel;
> Every man did what was right in his own eyes.
> *Judges 17:6 & 21:25 & 18:1 NASB*

As a pastor of 30 years, I fully understand the negative interpretation of the above scripture. It is almost always quoted by pastors as;

BAD: Being FREE to do what you feel is right…
GOOD: Being MADE to do what is "right" by a King…

As a pastor of a Bible believing church, I quoted this in the context of doing what we think is right versus doing what God says is right. A good foundational truth that Christians should let God be God and tell us what is right and wrong; don't make up our own moral code.

As I misquoted this scripture for a good purpose (as the head elder of our church aristocracy), I never asked myself what was the context. Was I for the system of the Kings of Israel or the government of *The Times of the Judges*? The context shows that God preferred men having the freedom to do what was right, once He had told them what was right. God was against Israel having a king – even when that king was King David; a man after God's own heart.

As much as *The Times of the Judges* is an affront to my Western World view of organization, efficiency and a need to have things well defined, God did not have a problem with the mess. The messiness of this time, that God so loved is the way self-rule works. Dictatorships really are more efficient but God was not for totalitarianism.

Once the nation of Israel's boundaries had been set and the Law of Moses had been established as the law of the land, we begin to see the practical establishment of government in *The Times of the Judges*. This system included the following government concepts.

A National Value System

The nation had been given God's set of pronouncements from Moses. These laws were divided into many statements of what is right and wrong. The details on how to treat animals, workers, and members of your family, were detailed by God's wisdom.

These laws set a common and accepted framework of what was right, wrong and how to deal with the law breaker. The practical application of these laws, by men finding how to maintain a free but ordered society is called *The Times of the Judges.*

Small Local Government
Individual Rights Protected

The elders of the city would sit in the gate and judge, when there was a dispute. Using the Law, they would determine what was right and wrong and how to proceed. If something fell outside the normal framework, they would judge in the spirit of the law.

Rules were expanded but the ruling may only be applied once, since the Law of Moses was the final arbitrator. Elders were related, literally to those in the city. The Elders of the city were either respected by their past dealings with the community or suspect by past failures. The national judge was given authority to overrule a city's elder ruling.

Regional (State) Governments
12 Separate Tribes

The Nation had been divided into 12 regional tribes, separate from the tribe of Levi. The city elders who carried seasoned authority came together as a "tribe." These regional governments made decisions for the whole tribe. The tribes (or states) had separate autonomy but were unified by being one nation under God.

National Secular Government

The nation had a special protection by God from its waring neighbors. When they decided to walk away from God, war broke out as this protection was lifted. God would appoint a National Judge to lead an army, rescue the nation and lead them back to righteousness.

The secular national government was limited. The stories show that national defense and interstate disputes was the main area of the national judges.

Separation of the Religious and the Secular

In *The Times of the Judges* there were three expressions of secular government; City Elders; Regional Leaders; National Judges. Eli, a high priest, from the tribe of Levi was the only case when the religious government was combined with the secular judges.

The national religious duties were performed by the God established non-profit group of Levitical Priests. The Priesthood oversaw and maintained the religious worship of the nation. The enforcement, of religious rules and secular law that defined the rules of human interaction was administered separately.

The times of Eli, the High Priest and Eli the national judge combined the authority of the secular and the religious. The abuse of power of Eli's sons would not have happened if the separation of the secular and religious had been maintained. It was under Eli that the system of government became exploitive and finally broke down, even after God's intervention in the story of the national judge, Samuel.

Most cults or other religious communities that mix secular and religious governmental power find similar abuses as we see with Eli and his sons. This separation did not separate God from the secular. This was a separation of human duties and human institutions to guard against human abuses. This same separation was included by our founders as a wise practice of government. This separation was not a freedom from God or the mention of God, but a freedom from the abuses that happen when authority is too centralized.

No Freedom FROM Religion

Spiritual and religious duties were delegated by God to the Levites. Levites had not received a secular inheritance of land. The rest of the nation had received land and homes as an inheritance from God's promises to Abraham. God wanted the Levites to be treated differently from the rest of the nation.

God established a national non-profit organization. The practice of worship, prayer and helping the poor were a part of the Israel's fabric, from the beginning of the nation.

City State / Tribal / Theocracy

A shallow review of Israel's *Times of the Judges*, may lead a person to believe that the stories are just a reflections of the ancient cultures. Was Israel a Religious State; a Primitive Tribal construct; or just some form of organic, family based cultural expression of government?

Since we have faith that the Bible is true, then we must also believe that God was doing something in this 500 year period of Israel's history. A closer look shows that Israel was the only ancient nation where the dynamics of Aristotle's three forms of Good Government appear. A limited National King-like figure (the judges), an Aristocracy (city elders) and the Republic – each man given the responsibility to do what is right.

I do not think it is a coincidence that Aristotle and the United States' founding fathers developed similar views of righteous government. They both used the Bible as their guide.

In Review, God created a National system that included:
1. A national set of laws
2. A voluntary national moral code
3. Small and limited government with individual rights
4. Regional governments autonomous from one another
5. Limited national government for security & interstate concerns
6. Separation of religious authority and secular authority
7. No ban on religious expression throughout society
8. National safety net - administered locally.

What Should We Do?

We can't go back to *The Times of the Judges*. Nor do we need to implement a specific type of government. Christianity can exist and even thrive in all government systems. But since we have some say over our government in the United States, we might consider implementing the wisdom of God's choices.

God Tells Us His Choice of Government

When it comes to politics, Christians usually fall into one of the following four groups.

1. The Isolationist
2. The King Seekers
3. The Government is the Answer Crowd
4. The Reformers

The Isolationist

Let the world go to Hell in a handbasket. Some sincere Christians do not care what the secular government does. They think they will live separate from the world and raise their children in God's teaching without being impacted. This naïve Christian attitude is usually only found in the United States. The rest of the world, each day pray similar prayers of the Apostle Paul; that they will be left free to serve God, without harassment.

I moved my family to 15 acres in the middle of nowhere when I was young and I sympathize with this position. It would be great to live totally separate from the world, but it is NOT Biblical. The Apostle Paul understood that freedom comes partially from the expression of government being righteous and stable.

> First of all, then, I urge that entreaties *and* prayers, petitions *and* thanksgivings, be made on behalf of all men, for kings and all who are in authority, so that we may lead a tranquil and quiet life in all godliness and dignity. This is good and acceptable in the sight of God our Savior, who desires all men to be saved and to come to the knowledge of the truth. *I Timothy 2:1-3 NASB*

The King Seekers

There are many Christians today that are seeking a King, as Israel did. Of course, we call these kings Presidents or Senators. When the citizens of a nation are looking for a king, they get King Saul most of the time. They get leaders who confidently make sweeping statements of certainty. Cult leaders also make black and white sweeping pronouncements. Instead of the humility that a good leader needs, these "kings" act as if they can solve all our problems.

As Christians, we do not have to look for a human savior. We already have one. We should ask God for wise leaders and fight for limited government. We should also look for moral men who want the same type of government as *The Times of the Judges*. But electing a Christian is not the answer. We do not need a Christian King. We need men of integrity; with leadership skills; communications skills to win people; and men with the ability and boldness to speak.

Government Is the Answer

These Christians sincerely believe that, "If only we get the right laws, we will have better government." We may need some secular answers to some passing problems. But what we really need is a reformation in how citizens relate to their government. We do not need better laws, we need better citizens. If we believe that God understood human government, then we should believe that the hope for our nation is returning to God's preferences. Looking to government to be the answer to most of our problems is futile.

The Reformer and Revivalist

If I shut up the heavens so that there is no rain, or if I command the locust to devour the land, or if I send pestilence among My people, and My people who are called by My name humble themselves and pray and seek My face and turn from their wicked ways, then I will hear from heaven, will forgive their sin and will heal their land. *II Chronicles 7:13-14 NASB*

"Yet even now," declares the LORD,
"Return to Me with all your heart,
And with fasting, weeping and mourning;
And rend your heart and not your garments."
Now return to the LORD your God,
For He is gracious and compassionate,
Slow to anger, abounding in lovingkindness
And relenting of evil. *Joel 2:12-13 NASB*

God Tells Us His Choice of Government

This is the only long-term hope for our nation. To return to a limited government republic, we will need to fight the tide to turn our nation into a BAD Democracy. We must start repenting from our trust in men, instead of God. We do not need a Christian King. We need God's favor.

I pastored a church in a conservative area of Southern California. That might sound strange to anyone who lives in California, but our Republican representatives in State and Federal government have tried to hold the line against ever increasing government intrusions.

So I was amazed when I attended a town hall meeting with one of these conservative state representatives. Every question from the 150 people attending was a question about what the representative was going to do for them. Everyone who spoke had a special interest and had come to the town hall meeting with their hat in the hand, looking for more "free" money.

I went away from this meeting with great sadness. Even our conservative leaders now regularly apologize for, "Congress not getting enough done." It is stated as a fact that government is the answer to our problems. Christians who want small, limited government and know the dangers of totalitarianism no longer articulate their principles clearly.

It is time for all Christians to add another fight to our two main moral issues. We should add the fight for our freedom from BAD Democracy.

4

Liberty, Money & The Bible
The Rightness of Free Markets

Those who try to justify democratic socialism make the argument that democracy is a governmental system and socialism is an economic system. They say you can be for the self-rule of the democracy and also have socialism. Milton Friedman disagreed.

> …such a view is a delusion, that there is an intimate connection between economics and politics, that only certain combinations of political and economic arrangements are possible, and that in particular, a society which is socialist cannot also be democratic, in the sense of guaranteeing individual freedom.[5]

Milton Friedman makes a clear argument in *Capitalism and Freedom* that the decoupling of a free economic system with a free governmental system is impossible. When the government goes beyond limited regulations it takes freedom away from someone.

The title of this book is tongue and cheek. Obviously, God is above all governments and financial systems. God is obviously above all of mankind's affairs. The title should have asked, "Does God want men to be free to own assets and buy and sell as they choose? OR does God want a small group of men to decide how, when and where most people can buy and sell?" That was a little long for a title, but that is the question.

As a pastor, I found myself misquoting one scripture from Paul's writing to Timothy. This scripture continues to be misquoted regularly, since the older King James Version has the slightly different interpretation as the original.

---

[5] Friedman, Milton (2009-02-15). Capitalism and Freedom: Fortieth Anniversary Edition (p. 8). University of Chicago Press. Kindle Edition.

> For the love of money is the root of **all** evil
> *I Timothy 6:10* **Older KJV**

Now most translations have changed this passage to accurately describe the temptation that men face when it comes to "the love of money."

> For the love of money is a root of
> **All sorts** (*or all kinds*) of evil...
> *NASB, NKJV, NLT, HCSB*

Money is just money. But the love of money is not the root of ALL evil, but it is the root of all sorts of evil. Money can do great things for God and bring great rewards from God, as seen in the story of the woman that gave one cent in Mark 12.

The morality of money is a big subject and there have been many sermons preached upon the subject. But have we heard a sermon about the *love of money* and how it effects governments and politicians? If individuals can sin with money, should we view bureaucrats and politicians differently? We could paraphrase the above scripture?

> For the politician's love of money
> is a root of all sorts of evil...

The Rich Neighbor Problem
The 10th Commandment

> "You shall not covet your neighbor's house; you shall not covet your neighbor's wife or his male servant or his female servant or his ox or his donkey or anything that belongs to your neighbor." *Exodus 20:17 NASB*

The 10th commandment is unique. It has more detail than most of the other commandments. It was as if God was saying, "OK, don't try to wriggle out of this one. Let Me make this crystal clear." It is the only commandment that has nothing to do with what you do. In all other commandments your actions are judged.

If you want to murder someone, but rein yourself in and don't murder, you have been obedient to the commandment. If you are tempted to commit adultery but don't commit adultery, you have been obedient to God's moral law. But the unrighteous attitudes of covetousness, leads to other bad and evil acts.

The Tenth speaks to your attitude toward your neighbor's assets. It is not talking about stealing your neighbors stuff. That is the 8th Commandment, "You shall not steal." God knew that humanity and their relationship to the physical world would be an important area of morality. He knew the temptation that humans would have when they did not have as much as someone else. Many sinful actions are birthed in the mind and heart. God is highlighting that coveting is one that should be avoided, period.

So God spelled it out for us.
> You shall not covet your neighbor's house;
> You shall not covet your neighbor's wife
> or his male servant
> or his female servant
> or his ox
> or his donkey

And just to be very, very clear God ends the commandment with, "or anything that belongs to your neighbor."

Coveting what other people have is NOW encouraged. We call it the need for "social justice," or "wage equality." This commandment takes away the moral foundation of communism, socialism, democratic socialism and any other form of government that addresses the "Rich Neighbor" problem by taking his assets.

Is Ambition Coveting?

Since history shows that free markets produce more innovation, more inventions and more production than any other system, this is an honest question to ask. Christian Luddites argue against the Liberty of Money with this argument; since coveting is wrong, so are the other emotions that drive us to have more are also wrong.

As a young man, I lived on 15 acres in a remote area of California that did not have electricity. I had to pay $11,000 to run Edison's lines one half mile to my house. This 2 year adventure made me very ambitious for the things that other people take for granted. When I flipped the switch on my bedroom wall, in the middle of the night nothing happened, until I turned the generator on.

Knowing that there was a better way to live, I really desired to live like my neighbors lived. Was I sinning when I was driven to dig a three foot deep trench for a half mile? Was I sinning when I desired what others had? Or was I working hard to improve my family's living conditions?

If ambition drives me to want other people's stuff, it is called Selfish Ambition. Socialism encourages everyone to desire other people's stuff. If ambition drives me to want to obtain things by sinful means, it would be considered Sinful Ambition. But Good Ambition drives me to better my life and my family's lives. And sometimes good ambition may drive me to bless the whole world with new inventions, new cures for diseases or just an easier way to wash dishes.

Being a Motivator to Do Good Works

>...and let us consider how to stimulate one another to love and good deeds... *Hebrews 10:24 NASB*

A friend and his wife, from the East Coast came to me in the first few years that I was pastoring a small church in Southern California. They told one of the Elders later, that they thought they could start a church too. They were older than me and as a new pastor, I stumbled in many ways. I feel they thought, "If he can do it, so can we."

There is an East Coast church that exists today, because someone saw me doing something and thought they could probably do it better. Praise God. Maybe someone will read this book and think, "I can write a book better than that." Freedom to pursue new things, without having to ask permission creates an atmosphere of innovation. Our present church should encourage Healthy Ambition and spur one another on to GOOD WORKS.

Ambition is a God Given Attribute

Let nothing be done through selfish ambition or conceit, but in lowliness of mind let each esteem others better than himself. Let each of you look out not only for his own interests, but also for the interests of others.
Philippians 2:3-4 NKJV

Because God has given us the ability to dream, plan and work toward goals, he exhorts us to not be selfish in our ambition. Some Christians become Luddites and seek to not have creativity or improvements by quoting this scripture, as if ALL ambition is wrong. But it is because God has given us drive and ambition that we must be encouraged to not only improve our own circumstances but also the circumstances of others.

Philippians 2:3-4 above is actually the definition of Moral Capitalism. When someone seeks to improve others circumstances, they sometimes create a business where others can also benefit from the improvement. That business, when successful expands and helps even more people.

The ability to remain content and dissatisfied at the same time is a special human characteristic. We should follow the Apostle Paul's exhortation to be content in whatever circumstance we find ourselves in. (Philippians 4:11). But always working to be divinely driven to be faithful with the gifts we have been given; a Divine Discontentment.

When most animals are hungry they find something to eat and then decide to take a nap. When a human is hungry he finds something to eat, but then thinks about his meals for next week and if he is a Christian whether his neighbor will have enough to eat, too.

The Justice of Free Enterprise

Social Justice is a misnomer. When the term Social Justice is used, it actually means unearned charity. Full justice is when everyone gets exactly what they deserve, in every case, every time. Jesus mentions this principle of pure justice when He quoted Exodus 21.

> An eye for an eye, and a tooth for a tooth ...
> *Mathew 5:38 NASB*

> Eye for eye, tooth for tooth, hand for hand,
> foot for foot, burn for burn,
> wound for wound, bruise for bruise.
> *Exodus 21:24-25 NASB*

Secular justice means the punishment should always fit the crime. This seeking justice in every circumstance is the foundation of a stable government. When the authorities in any nation are viewed as unjust, the people begin to rebel and find ways to game or pervert the system.

What would a life of full justice look like?

You travel down the highway at 70 MPH in a 55 MPH speed zone; you get a ticket – every time. You cheat on your taxes and gain a $200 deduction that you do not deserve; the $200 is taken back by the entity that you cheated, plus a penalty for trying to cheat. You give a stranger a gift and somehow the same amount plus interest comes back to you...

We want the Secular Justice System to always administer justice. But we also want mercy to be mixed with this justice for ourselves. We want a full accounting and punishment for the person who stole our child's bicycle. But when we go before the court we want mercy.

If a financial system was 100% JUST, everyone would be paid according to the value they produced in their jobs. Every job would have a complicated formula to determine how much the factory worker had produced. One person may earn twice as much as the person next to him, because he produced twice as much. Another formula would apply to each service worker. Taking long lunches or breaks would always cut into the worker's paycheck.

If a financial system was 100% JUST, every job would, by necessity be a "piece part," job. If a professional basketball player played in a game that it was determined 20,000 more people came to watch him. He would be paid $5,000,000 more than his teammates minus $500,000 overhead. The hotdog worker that sold 500 hotdogs at the same game and made 95 cents profit per hot dog may only go home with $50.00.

Didn't the hot dog vendor work as hard as the professional basketball player? This question cannot be answered. The professional basketball player worked hundreds of hours to be a good basketball player. The hot dog vendor may have made it to work 5 minutes before starting with a hangover from drinking too much the night before.

As you can see having a financial system that rewards everyone 100% JUSTLY is unworkable. Only God could figure out what and why your paycheck was a certain amount. With this inability to determine the value of things, the Law of Moses establishes justice about the punitive damages of stolen business assets.

> "If a man steals an ox or a sheep and slaughters it or sells it,
> he shall pay five oxen for the ox
> and four sheep for the sheep.
> *Exodus 22:1 NASB*

Until God gets into the paycheck business, the next best way to have a JUST system is the free market system. Everyone is free to decide if the wage or price is fair. Successful businesses always do this. Paying someone too much or selling something too cheap only works until the business goes bankrupt.

But some people see the difference between the hot dog vendor and the professional basketball player's compensation and mistakenly label this difference in pay as an injustice. The opposite is true. In both cases they had the right to choose their compensation as determined by the free market. Skill, training, dependability, profit increases all influence the paycheck of both.

But some well-intentioned Christians, even leaders, sadly proclaim "This should not happen in a country as rich as ours." It really sounds good to rail against anything and finish with the phrase, "in a country as rich as ours." This non-argument is made over and over again by men who do not have any other system that would be more JUST.

A Just Government

I have included a doctrinal statement on "turning the other cheek," in Appendix I, since this passage is misquoted and misused to justify Christians seeking Social Justice (mercy). Misquoting Jesus, we are told to not seek, *"An Eye for an Eye."* But in matters of government, legal courts and the application of laws, Jesus did not advocate anarchy or a sliding scale of justice.

Let us look at an example. I buy a piece of property and build a house on it. A decade later, my neighbor goes to the court and says, "Give me some of Greg's property. I need 25 feet of his south border." The court then decides that although I own the property and have all legal rights, my neighbor is poor and he needs it more than I do. And because I am rich, the court also gives him the garage I built on the south border.

Was justice served? Or was justice perverted? When a court or a government decides that the law is going to be bent anytime it seems "fair," the rule of law no longer matters. Civilization breaks down and how you are treated depends upon who is in control that week.

In 1973 President Nixon put price controls on oil reacting to the Arab Oil Embargo. Politicians did not have to stand in line all day (only on even days) to fill their cars with gas so they could go to work, as I did. I bought a motorcycle to drive to work to save gas and to be allowed to buy gas on any day. Wage and price controls always hurt the poor and lower middle class because they create shortages. Thomas Sowell says that, "Price controls are essentially lies about supply and demand."[6]

These lies about what things are worth distort the markets. Christians should be against all perversion of the markets by government. We should shine a light on these lies and confront the liars with the truth. We should also recognize that all attempts at distorting the markets by the government is not just deceptive but takes our freedom to choose.

---

[6] Sowell, Thomas (2011-10-04). The Thomas Sowell Reader (p. 70). Basic Books. Kindle Edition.

Thomas Sowell continues. "...government planning is not an alternative to chaos. It is a preemption of other people's plans."[7]

All government intervention in our financial markets takes away someone's freedom to choose. Capitalism is the only system that is FAIR or allows as much justice as possible every time; because both parties agree upon the terms of the transaction. All other systems, grant someone else the power to decide (plan) what each individual can buy, sell or earn. The individual cannot choose but only agree to what the central planners determine is JUST.

Recognizing the Cause of Scarcity

I love to go shopping with my friends from Australia. "There are so many choices," they exclaim. They are amazed and love shopping in the United States.

Another pastor friend, from Australia buys a few items that are overpriced or not available in Australia on each trip. Then he sells the items when he gets back to Australia and finances his trip with the profits. Of course this is cheating (gaming) the Australian Democratic Socialist System. But everyone who lives in an over-controlled system learns how to break the rules, even when they are a pastor.

Most people in the world do not know what it is like to have our freedom of choice. Even in a relatively free society such as Australian, the lack of goods and services takes away their opportunity to choose. The higher tax rates take away the opportunity to buy with the money they have earned. Many products aren't available, anyway.

After spending time in Australia, I realized that they did not know how slow their internet service is compared to the United States or how much more they pay for their slow service. The deception of socialism is that they don't know what they don't have. I love the people of Australia, but their choice of socialism maintains a deception; they are deceived because they never know what could be.

---

[7] Sowell, Thomas (2011-10-04). The Thomas Sowell Reader (p. 46). Basic Books. Kindle Edition.

Star Trek or the Bible

In Star Trek, humanity has progressed to greater and greater levels of righteousness through education and evolution. Humanity has evolved to the place that government (the Federation) exists without monetary motives. Men just want to do the right thing. As Christians, we reject this view of mankind. This is the atheist's only hope for humanity.

Star Trek never explains why everyone is always attacking the Enterprise and trying to kill Captain James T. Kirk. I guess humans have evolved and the rest of the universe is still trying to steal each other's stuff. This naïve view of mankind is regularly applied when men preach against the evils of the Free Enterprise System.

Good intentioned Christians lament, "There must be a better way." But never come up with one. If they are against capitalism, then they are for some type of a CONTROLLED system. So we should ask ourselves, "Who is going to control the money?"

It is time for Christians to stand and fight for freedom – to fight for the FREE Enterprise System.

5
Complaints about Capitalism

Those who have a problem with free markets complain about things that sound rational at first. Some of these complainers are Christians. If capitalism is bad, then it is our mission, as Christians to change the system to something better. But if the complaints themselves are lies then the complainers are deceived.

Many who complain about the immorality of free markets feel that money, in and of itself is a corrupting factor of the human heart. They misquote scripture. *"Money is the root of all evil."* Therefore money is inherently bad.

The complainers then make an argument that cannot be argued with. Their theory seems to explain everything. As Charles Krauthammer once said on Fox News, "A theory that explains everything, explains nothing." Here is how the argument against money goes.

Men do criminal acts because they are poor. If they had better jobs or more opportunity they would be better men. But on the other hand those who have large amounts of money are also, mostly bad. They are greedy and miserly. They abuse the poor and steal from those who are less fortunate. So if you are poor, your lack of money makes you sinful and if you are rich, your excess money makes you sinful. It would seem that all sinful acts can be traced back to money or the lack there of.

Christians believe Romans 3:23.

> ...for all have sinned and fall short of the glory of God *NASB*

So the Christian starts with a different opinion about money than the anti-capitalist. We believe that money may have an influence on men's hearts. But all men are sinful, no matter how much money they have or don't have. Sin comes from a man's heart condition and not his present life circumstances.

Since atheists do not believe in anything beyond the material world, their "doctrines" must attribute all sin to economic or other materialistic roots. And most of those who originally formed the anti-capitalist complaints of this chapter were atheists.

Complaint I
Free Enterprise Enables Large Scale Sin

I started with this complaint about people having more money than they need, not because it is the most quoted or the worst complaint. I started here because this is a common belief of sincere Christians. Many fundamental Christians have a big problem with the many sins of America and draw an incorrect connection to America's wealth.

19th and 20th Century Genocide seems to be far away. Totalitarian, atheistic governments, who oppress their citizens, are seldom mentioned. China's forced late term abortions are on the other side of the world. So we hear sermons about how the "American Dream" is bad; or how Americans spend more on dog food than missions; or how few really give their fair share.

I agree with sincere Christians who call Americas to righteous behavior. But attacking capitalism, the system that has produced the wealth seems to be counter-productive. It also plays into the atheist's game plan by confusing the Christian into immoral and amoral political positions. These doctrines have their foundation in Materialism.

By definition, *temptation* is something that we want to do but shouldn't do. When men have more money they will have more opportunity to sin but not more temptations. Since a poor man and a rich man have the same sinful heart, they both struggle with temptations. A poor man can be greedy and a rich man can be generous. A rich man can covet his neighbor's wife and a poor man can obey the Ten Commandments.

I believe that Christians, who desire less sinful behavior in their society, should take a political stance to keep markets as free as possible. This may seem counter intuitive, but limited government, which maintains free markets, is the most desirable system for the following 2 reasons.

REASON 1 - There are always more bad people than good people.

> "In everything, therefore, treat people the same way you want them to treat you, for this is the Law and the Prophets.
> "Enter through the narrow gate; for the gate is wide and the way is broad that leads to destruction, and there are many who enter through it. For the gate is small and the way is narrow that leads to life, and there are few who find it. *Matthew 7:12-14 NASB*

Immediately following the above verse paraphrased "Do unto others as you would have them do unto you," is a verse that tells why limiting all men's power and ability to do evil is the best approach to politics. Good men seek positions of power and wealth. Evil men also seek these same positions of control and influence. Our problem is that there will always be more bad men than good men. And there are some really evil men mixed in with the bad group that is going through the wide gate of Matthew 7, above.

Therefore, wouldn't it be better to limit the scope of all government and allow free markets so that each man may by his own work and skill create wealth. Free markets maintained by a limited government functioning within Ten Commandment rules; no cheating, no lying, no fraud, no stealing; restricts the all men, including evil men.

An evil man can do much more damage to humanity when political systems give him vast authority. Since there are more evil men seeking to do this, it is better to not develop politics that put a lot of power into a few men's hands.

REASON 2 - God allows free choice and the consequences of sin that comes from those choices.

God's sadness over the sinful condition of man does not motivate him to restrict most of men's endeavors. It is the arrogant atheist's position to work to see a heaven on earth, by controlling most buying and selling. Giving all men the freedom to sin, also gives good men the opportunity to do good works.

Complaint II
The Rich Get Richer

The statistics prove this widely held belief as false. The wealth of households and individuals is always changing from year to year. Thomas Sowell explains why "The Rich Get Richer" is a lie.

> ... [T]he statistical category "top one percent" of income recipients has received a growing share of the nation's income in recent years—while the actual flesh-and-blood taxpayers who were in that category in 1996 actually saw their income go down by 2005.
>
> What makes it possible for both these apparently contradictory statements to be true is that more than half of the people who were in the top one percent at the beginning of the decade were no longer there at the end. As their incomes declined, they dropped out of the top one percent.
>
> The same principle applies in the lower income brackets. The share of the national income going to the statistical category "lowest 20 percent" of taxpayers has been declining somewhat over the years but the actual flesh-and-blood human beings who were in the bottom 20 percent in 1996 had their incomes increase by an average of 91 percent by 2005. This nearly doubling of their incomes took more than half of them out of the bottom 20 percent category.[8]

Due to free enterprise, people have an opportunity to move from the lowest income categories to the highest categories. With hard work, determination and some luck, those in lower categories can even bump the higher earners out of their category.

This upward movement of working class people is one of the reasons most of the statistics that you hear on the nightly news are twisted. Thomas Sowell calls these twisted numbers "Snap Shot Statistics."

---

[8] Sowell, Thomas (2011-03-22). Economic Facts and Fallacies: Second Edition (p. 140). Basic Books. Kindle Edition

The truth is that in free markets some of the rich get poorer; many of the poor get richer; the middle class becomes richer. The wealthy retire, falling out of the income statistics, confusing the numbers. Instead of quoting a lie, we should quote the truth, "The poor become richer."

Complaint III
The Poor Get Poorer

Once again the facts dispute the common belief that Capitalism oppresses and exploits the poor. This axiom has been repeated so many times, sometimes from the pulpit that the lie has grown into a Christian axiom in some churches.

In 1993, I drove through the garbage dumps just outside Manila Philippines. The road stretched for miles with 20 foot high mounds of garbage as far as you could see. Living in the garbage dumps of Manila were the poorest of the poor. Little children played at the edges of the mounds.

Arthur Brooks' Prager University course *Myths, Lies and Capitalism* states the following.

> Since 1970, the percentage of the world's population living on the equivalent of less than a dollar a day has fallen by more than 80 percent. This was not the result of foreign aid or U.N. development projects. It was the spread of free enterprise that achieved this miracle.
>
> In China alone, free trade and foreign investment - investment not aid - lifted 400 million Chinese out of abject poverty in just the 20 years between 1981 and 2001. There has never been a force for helping the poor that has come close to free enterprise. [9]

In 2015 there was good news. The headline at the Washington Post.com read, *"For the first time, less than 10 percent of the world is living in extreme poverty, World Bank says."*

---

[9] prageru.com/courses/economics/myths-lies-and-capitalism; Arthur Brooks

The chart showed a line slanted downward describing those living on less than $1.90 a day; in 1990 - 37.1% of the World's population and in 2015 - 9.6%. Reporter Adam Taylor writes in this Post article:

> The new figures are certainly remarkable when you consider that just 25 years ago more than a third of the world was living in extreme poverty, according to the Bank's figures. Despite the rising population all around the world, there are less than half the number of people living in extreme poverty in 2015 than there were in 1990.[10]

In the last few decades, there has not been any giant government program; no non-profit charity; no scientific break-through. What has happened is the totalitarian governments of the world have realized that allowing financial markets more freedom creates wealth. Dictators and tyrants have released some control of their economies, allowing the poor to work and keep more of what they earn. Think what could happen if governments were stable, limited in their authority and had Christian values.

Globalization

Free trade in developing countries has created this rising tide of Capitalism. Free trade has allowed the poorest of the world to be lifted out of poverty. This Globalization of the markets has helped millions of the extreme poor. But as this has happened, there has been an outcry by some in the United States to keep the cheap foreign products from being sold here. High paying jobs have been lost to these poor people.

This myopic view of the world is not a Christian view, yet big union Christians try to take poor people's jobs, to save their own high paying jobs. This is the definition of greed. They do not want cheap goods competing with their higher priced goods and truly are becoming richer on the backs of the extreme poor of the world. Maybe, out of ignorance, they try to use government to control world markets. Each regulation and tariff that they lobby congress to pass distorts the markets. Cheap

---

[10] www.washingtonpost.com/news/worldviews/wp/2015/10/05/

products help the poor and middle class of our nation. Yet socialists and crony capitalists in the United States push for controlled markets.[11]

It is ironic that globalization, which has helped so many really poor people throughout the world has caused an unholy alliance with socialists and religious people. They do not see their political position as greedy. They do not see that it is hurting the extreme poor.

But they cannot hide from the self-centeredness of their position. They are all looking out for number one by trying to take freedom from financial transactions. Instead of preaching against those Greedy Corporations, why don't we hear preaching against Greedy American Workers who stand against globalization?

Household Income vs Individual Income

If you listen to the government, you would think there was no difference in America and in the garbage dumps of Manila. The headlines are always the same, *The Poor Are Getting Poorer*. Household incomes have gone down over the last decades. Capitalism is failing. Capitalism doesn't work for the middle class or poor.

But wait. Thomas Sowell once again helps us see how the government has pulled a slight of hand with the numbers. As a nation becomes wealthier, the individuals in that nation find more and more independence. They make choices to move out and live on their own.

This freedom to have your own HOUSEHOLD, live on your own and support yourself is a good thing. There is nothing wrong with the elderly moving in with their children, and there is nothing wrong with young adults staying at home. But as we become wealthier, the young move out and the elderly stay independent in their own homes.

But when the household is small – say only having one person's income counted as household income the numbers tell a sad story, of stagnate Capitalist failure. If a household has three income earners being counted, it has more income. But if we measure the real income

---

[11] Mad About Trade: Why Main Street America should Embrace Globalization First Edition by Daniel T. Griswold Chapter 9

of individuals, we see a different story. Thomas Sowell's book *Economics Facts and Fallacies* brings clarity to this propaganda about household income versus individual income.

> As of 2007, for example, black household income was lower than Hispanic household income, even though black per capita income was higher than Hispanic per capita income, because black households average fewer people than Hispanic households.

> Similarly, Asian American household income was higher than white household income, even though white per capita income was higher than Asian American per capita income, because Asian American households average more people.[12]

Sowell continues in his book siting the U.S. Bureau of the Census, *"Changes in Median Household Income: 1969 to 1996,"* that individual income increased 51% over the period while household income increased only 6%.[13]

The poor are not getting poorer, even though the government chooses to use the negative numbers to try to convince us that capitalism is not working. The real statistics show we are doing much better than they would like us to know.

The Poor in America Live Above the Poverty Line

The poor of America spend more than their income each year. That's right – read that again. The poor of America spend more money than they have in income each year. How is this possible? It is not that the poor has a lot of credit cards. The government cooks the books. The Federal income statistics of those who live below the poverty line do not record any money or service given to them from any government program. Their actual income is recorded 78% lower than the resources they actually receive and use. Thomas Sowell continues:

---

[12] Sowell, Thomas (2011-03-22). Economic Facts and Fallacies: Second Edition (p. 141). Basic Books. Kindle Edition
[13] Sowell, Thomas (2011-03-22). Economic Facts and Fallacies: Second Edition (p. 257). Basic Books. Kindle Edition.

Given such disparities between the economic reality and the alarming statistics, it is much easier to understand such apparent anomalies as the fact that Americans living below the official poverty level spend far more money than their incomes—as their income is defined in statistical studies.[14]

As a pastor, I had people in my congregation who had income each month below the poverty line. They had one or two cars; a Section 8 housing allowance in a good area of the city; an EBT card for food; more than one free cell phone; and enough resources to raise their children in the same circumstances as the average middle class family in our community.

Their income level was low and this qualified them for Federal, State, County and sometimes City help. The government's LIE is that they are living in poverty. Ironically, because of our present level of government help, and excluding the mentally ill and addicted, the poor are not poor, by American standards.

There has been much discussion on whether the *War on Poverty* has been lost, due to this propaganda. This brings us to a statistical dichotomy that big spending politicians and socialists do not want the general public to understand. If they admit the programs they initiate are successful, they will have no other reason to ask for more programs. They must never admit the war on poverty is won. The government has actually won the war but refuses to tell anyone, about their victory.

Chapter 12 explores in detail God's view of the correct National Safety Net. Christians will continue to help the poor, no matter what the government reports. But we should not participate in this deception. I have heard many misleading stats quoted in prayers to God. Sincere Christians should be more discerning and question the numbers on poverty; the number of homeless, how many kids go to bed hungry; how many children need to be adopted. A lie to make a point is still a LIE.

---

[14] Sowell, Thomas (2011-03-22). Economic Facts and Fallacies: Second Edition (pp. 144-145). Basic Books. Kindle Edition.

Our Christian approach is to give money, time and help to rescue the poor. But it is not Christian to go with a gun to our neighbor's house and rob him to give to the poor; nor should the government.

Capitalism is the poor man's only long-term hope to escape poverty.

Complaint IV
Free Markets Are Not Fair

It is said that justice is equality, and so it is,
But not for all persons, only for those who are equal.
ARISTOTLE, POLITICS

Arthur Brooks, in his book *The Road to Freedom: How to Win the Fight for Free Enterprise,* tells a story. His students felt they were politically progressive and were very concerned about the FAIRNESS of the Free Market System.

Arthur Brooks says that by the middle of the course, it is obvious which students are working hard to get a top grade and the students who are not as motivated and are not working as hard.

The hard workers got lots of points on their tests and quizzes; their less motivated friends didn't. We all knew that the students with the highest point totals were working harder.... They might have been a bit brighter or already knew more about economics, but the real difference was how much they were studying.

I proposed that the class take a quarter of the points earned by the top half of the class and pass them on to the students in the lower half of the class. The students were in unanimous agreement that this was a stupid idea. Redistributing points earned on the basis of hard work and merit, simply so that students who didn't study could get a higher grade, would be completely unfair. Even students at the bottom thought the scheme was idiotic. [15]

---

[15] Brooks, Arthur C. (2012-05-08). The Road to Freedom: How to Win the Fight for Free Enterprise (p. 51). Basic Books. Kindle Edition.

At first glance, capitalism may seem unfair. But the truth is ALL redistribution of wealth through government intervention is UNFAIR. It may bring equality, but it is not FAIR equality. As the students in Brook's class reacted, so should all thinking citizens.

The definition of justice, fairness, charity and mercy has now changed depending upon a person's politics. As Christians, these words are not political rhetoric but a part of our values. We should not allow our language to be turned upside down. This redefining of words leads to confusion of the moral issues of our day. As a Christian, we are more sensitive to this perverting of the language, since we have been warned in the Bible.

> Woe to those who call evil good, and good evil;
> Who substitute darkness for light and light for darkness;
> Who substitute bitter for sweet and sweet for bitter!
> *Isaiah 5:20 NASB*

Our emotions seem to disconnect from our mental processes when we begin to define FAIRNESS. We see a baseball player making millions of dollars and the parking attendant making minimum wage, and our first response is that there is something wrong here. But after our first primal response, we should think through our emotions about the fairness and unfairness. Is it really UNFAIR to give someone with little skills a job at minimum wage? What is the alternative?

When we discuss justice in financial transactions, a just transaction is someone earning exactly what their actions are worth. A fully just wage is dependent upon:

> The ability of the employer to replace the worker
> The amount of workers who want to do the job
> The training that the job requires
> The skills that are needed to do the job
> The present condition of the economy's total jobs available
> The agreed upon contract between the employer and the worker.

Seeking justice in wages and prices becomes very complicated. If we really want FAIR or JUST wages, we would never institute a minimum wage. Since each job has many different factors which make it worth something to the employer and worth something to the worker.

Is The Minimum Wage FAIR?

On January 1ˢᵗ 2016 California minimum wage increased to $10.00 an hour. The increase has already hurt the poor, and only the poor. Those making $20 or $30 dollars an hour are not affected by this Wage - Lie propagated by California State Government. In three ways the poor are hurt by a high minimum wage.

1. Higher commodity prices for everyone including the poor
2. Fewer jobs available at the bottom
3. More skilled workers competing for low skilled positions

Higher Commodity Prices Hurt the Poor

I have hired minimum wage employees for decades in three different states, all with different minimum wages. The minimum wage increases have not hurt my business, because I raised my prices to keep the same profit margins. I assume the businesses I contract with also raise their prices. The middle class feel the pressure of rising prices but can tighten their belts and not eat at McDonalds as much. The rich don't feel the pinch of higher prices at all. But the poor will always feel the pain of price increases.

Fewer Jobs Hurt the Poor

When the government creates a lie in the wage market, the market reacts by finding a way to do the job in a way that aligns with the truth. I have begun buying machines to do what my employees use to do on as many jobs as possible. Twenty years ago I eliminated one full time job by buying a machine at a large facility. But now I can make more profit by letting machines do the work at smaller buildings, too.

Each machine robs someone of the hours they use to be paid to do the same job. At $10.00 an hour, the machine pays for itself in one month. The higher the minimum wage, the more intelligent the machine can be to compensate for the dollars already being spent to do the job. These machines do not get hurt on the job and do not require thousands of dollars in workers compensation insurance. And they don't use California's new mandatory three paid sick days a year.

Job Competition Hurts the Less Skilled

I now hire a different type of employee. When the minimum wage was lower, the people who applied for the jobs were mainly young people, just starting out and other unskilled groups. Many could not speak English and had little education. These groups still apply for my jobs. Their problem is that a $10.00 an hour job now has another applicant competing for the same job. This new applicant is someone with some skills; they usually speak English; they have a work history. Sometimes they do twice as much work as the former applicants. Who do you think will get the job?

My heart still goes out to the Spanish speaking grandmother who needs to work 3 hours a night and takes pride in her job. My heart still goes out to the young man trying to get his foot into the door and is willing to work at the bottom to make it higher up. But they seldom get a job because of the higher wage. California has priced them out of the market. Is that FAIR?

These unemployed workers use to take pride knowing that they had a job. It wasn't a great job, but it was a place that they could be rewarded for their efforts and paid for the value they created. Each week they looked at their pay check and felt a sense of accomplishment that they had earned money. They were successful at their jobs. Now they sit at home. Is that FAIR?

The Fewer Jobs Data

Seattle, San Francisco and Los Angeles city governments have all decided that it is better to not let markets set the minimum wage. The data is just starting to be compiled. Those who say that, lying to the markets can help workers, do not use the jobs data to make their argument. The Wall Street Journal reports:

> It's still early to know how the hikes are affecting the job market, but the preliminary data aren't good. Mark Perry of the

American Enterprise Institute, Adam Ozimek of Moody's Analytics and Stephen Bronars of Edgewood Economics reported last month that the restaurant and hotel industries have lost jobs in all three cities.

Mr. Bronars crunched the numbers and discovered that the "first wave of minimum wage increases appears to have led to the loss of over 1,100 food service jobs in the Seattle metro division and over 2,500 restaurant jobs in the San Francisco metro division."[16]

This article goes on to say that in 2014 the Federal Government studies showed that increasing the minimum wage would cut 500,000 jobs from the work force. It may feel good to think that our wages are all high, but lying to the markets will always result in a negative result.

Why Free Markets Are FAIRER

The key insight of Adam Smith's Wealth of Nations is misleadingly simple: if an exchange between two parties is voluntary, it will not take place unless both believe they will benefit from it. Most economic fallacies derive from the neglect of this simple insight, from the tendency to assume that there is a fixed pie that one party can gain only at the expense of another.[17]

As Christians our main concern should be that the markets set prices that are fair and that no one is forced, bullied, or intimidated to sell or buy something at an unjust price. So why would free markets always arrive at the FAIR price? Here are 3 reasons:

1. No one is hurt.

If two people decide to buy or sell something; if they see value and decide upon a price; then that transaction benefits both parties and hurts no one. At the writing of this book the Beatles original recording

---

[16] http://www.wsj.com/articles/a-post-labor-day-minimum-wage-hangover-1441667048

[17] Milton Friedman; Free to Choose (p. 13) Kindle Edition.

contract sold for $75,000. This piece of paper was worth that much money to someone, obviously not me. No one can say what the buyer would have done with the $75,000 if he had not won the auction. And no one can say what the seller will do with the $75,000. But this transaction did not hurt anyone.

2. A business only succeeds when it sells a lot of stuff.

When a business offers a product or service, it is trying to make a profit from more than one transaction. To have a successful business the seller must find a price that is acceptable to the buyer, over and over again.

A business may be able to fool a few people and charge a very high price for an item. If the price is set too high, two things will happen. First, someone will see an opportunity to supply the same item at a fair price. Second, the buyers will walk away from the high price, motivating the business to lower the price or go out of business. Excluding conmen, who should be arrested, the market quickly rewards the best price.

3. The crowd always sets the best price.

In 1906 a scientist visited a regional fair in West England. He saw a contest where people were guessing the weight of a fat ox. The crowd was full of many uneducated people. It also had a few farmers who could make accurate guesses.

The scientist decided to use this contest as an experiment. He felt the crowd would miss the ox's weight by a large amount, since most were non-farmers and uneducated. He gathered the slips that had been filled out and found 800 people had guessed. After throwing away 13 illegible tickets, he had 787 tickets. The average weight of the Ox, slaughtered and dressed was guessed to be 1197 lbs. After the ox was slaughtered and dressed the weight was 1198 lbs. The crowd together had missed by only one pound.[18]

---

[18] Surowiecki, James (2005-08-16). The Wisdom of Crowds . Knopf Doubleday Publishing Group. Kindle Edition.

A similar experiment with a large number of people guessing how many jelly beans are in a jar has been done many times. As long as the results are not impacted by outside information, the results remain the same. The average of the large crowd's guess is very close to the exact number. A large crowd always beats the experts.

When applied to free markets the crowd sets pricing and wages in each community. This crowd sourcing action is much more dependable than a few very, very smart people trying to find the right answer. Central controlled economies use the least accurate method of finding the FAIR price of goods and services. When the government intimidates, taxes, subsidizes or just puts on price controls, they always get it wrong. The experts always are less accurate than the large crowd; ALWAYS.

The expert's inaccurate markets develop bubbles and shortages. When the bubble bursts, it is blamed upon the markets. But in every case the government is responsible for missing the fair price and creating the distortion.

The question is not "What is fair?" The question is, "Who will decide the correct price or wage?"
1. Relatively average and sometimes below average politicians
2. Experts
3. Scientists
4. Presidents
5. The large crowd in the free market?

A correct price reflects the value accurately and is then FAIR by definition. Free markets interactions are the only way that the FAIR price for goods, services and wages can be set. And that is FAIR.

Complaint V
Duplication Causes Waste

The socialists among us say that we have too much duplication and that this duplication is wasteful. They state that having ten auto insurance companies advertising is wasteful and hurts the poor. They state that having 10 brands of ketchup in a grocery store is wasteful and hurts our economy.

They state something like this. "Why do we need so many _____?" They finish their argument with, "… we could have spent that money on something else. We could have used that money to help the poor or education or _____."

Let us look closer at this childlike view of economics. If a central controlled Ketchup Bureaucracy decides that having 3 choices of ketchup is quite enough, it puts out of business the other 7 companies. These 7 companies that are put out of business have workers, investors, vendors, and janitors who will all lose their jobs when the 3 "best" brands are selected.

You would think that if you owned a large ketchup company you would fight the establishment of the Federal Ketchup Bureaucracy. But this seldom happens in a Big Government Democracy. The large corporations begin positioning themselves to be picked as one of the top 3. It is easy to do business, when your competitors banned.

The bureaucracy in its great wisdom picks the 3 best companies, forcing a large disruption in the ketchup manufacturing sector and all the corresponding businesses from tomato farmers to vat suppliers. The three companies with less competition start to raise their prices and sell a lot of ketchup. But because the price goes up quicker, since it is not tied to wide economic events, people start to buy more mustard and less ketchup. The controlled commodity is still making a better profit margin but the companies are making less sells, so their profits are flat.

The Ketchup Bureaucracy sees what is happening and goes to congress for more authority to control the price, thinking they will help the poor keep up their ketchup consumption. It is not FAIR that the evil Ketchup Corporations are charging more for ketchup. No one blames the government, for enabling the 3 big companies to become bigger.

The three ketchup companies now see that they are not making as much total profit from their sells even with the higher prices, because of something called *The Economies of Scale*. Since they are not selling as much ketchup, the net profits for ketchup sales have gone down.

The government is pressuring them to not charge what they need to charge to make the same profit they made before the regulations went into effect. They cut their production down even more to try to find the "sweet spot," for the New Normal as far as ketchup prices are concerned.

The Great Ketchup Shortage of 2020

Now two things have happened because of the Central Planners. They have taken away the public's choices, especially the poor's choices. The poor use to buy the cheaper brands. The planners have created a shortage in the markets. Government blames the Free Markets. They will never admit that there restrictions have caused unemployment and less tax revenues to provide normal services.

Government duplication is bad. Free Market duplication is great.
We in the United States have become unware of one of the great benefits of our Free Enterprise System – Duplication; more choices, more competition, more business activity, more jobs.

This freedom to choose from a large selection has been created only by free markets suppling what people want and need. The markets will decide if there are too many Ketchup Companies.

Complaint VI
Capitalism Hurts The Environment

In 2015, Pope Francis complained that capitalism is ruining the environment and that unbridled capitalism is "The Dung of the Devil." His views could be classified as Christian Marxist, if there was such a thing. The Enemies of Capitalism, in Chapter 8 have the same view as Pope Francis. His opinion agrees with the atheists of the 20th Century.

Most human beings, including most capitalists want clean air, clean water and less human suffering from environmental catastrophes. Capitalists also want to be viewed as responsible community members; probably more than the average citizen, since their public persona may affect their profits. Hollywood's reactionary lies have convinced many Christians to view this issue as Evil Capitalist vs Courageous Bureaucrat. The truth is the Goliath of the story is the government.

Free Enterprise Provides Funds

The fact is that the richer the nation the less the environmental impact, as long as you compare apples with apples. Singapore compared to Indonesia; Hong Kong compared to any area of China; every comparison shows the same result.

Although the free market economies provide more goods and services per capita and consume more goods and services per capita, they also are more responsible with the environment. The enemies of free enterprise, including the pope when he talks about "unbridled capitalism," do not have any solution other than government control.

The facts show, that the solution to pollution is for the poorer countries to abandon their failed government controls and create free markets that do not let men steal, cheat or lie. As their country becomes richer, their environmental impact will be less.

Limited honest and representative government will allow the world's extreme poor to have electricity, sewer systems and food. Those, like the Pope, who take the position that capitalism hurts the environment, do not understand that they are locking the extreme poor into really bad living conditions. Capitalism does not make men choose between feeding their families and being environmentally responsible.

The church should give to the poor and ALSO work to free the world of Controlled Economies that lock their people into the poverty which ultimately hurts the environment.

Complaint VII
Wall Street Is Bad

This is not a book about investing. But the morality of the Stock Markets should be a concern to Christians. The Stock Markets are not in and of themselves evil any more than the supermarket that people visit regularly. Your local supermarket sells thousands of items each day. Your stock market also sells thousands of items each day. There are sinners shopping in our supermarkets and there are sinners trading in our stock markets.

Complaints about Capitalism

There are people trying to steal things at our supermarkets and there are insiders trading in the stock markets. Bernie Madoff stole over 50 billion dollars and was sentenced to 150 years in prison. But the Bernie Madoff story is not a story of how bad the stock markets of the world are. It is a story of how many people want to get rich faster than everyone else. It is also the story of how government regulations fail. Free market security works much better. A private security company would have stopped Madoff before he stole 50 Billion dollars.

4 Reasons We Need the Stock Markets

Reason 1
The Free Flow of Capital Helps Start New Businesses
Billionaire Home Depot co-founder, Ken Langone says that Home Depot could not be started in today's regulatory environment. Since the 2008 home mortgage meltdown, laws have been passed to over-regulate the stock market. Instead of seeing the futility of the government ability to WATCH investing, they made more laws. Instead of turning to Free Enterprise to solve the Madoff problem, they made more regulations that hinder free markets and will probably not catch the next Madoff. Home Depot employs 371,000. This type of business needs a very large amount of capital at the beginning stages. The stock markets are one of the few places this type of business can be capitalized.

Reason 2
Speculators Provide Liquidity
A market where you have no sellers or no buyers is a market that people soon stop visiting. What would happen if your neighborhood supermarket had apples, oranges, grapes but they were not selling them on the day that you visited?

The supermarket owner would post each day the items that were for sell that day. People would come to buy apples only to find that apples were not for sell that day. The supermarket owner wants to provide the items that his customers are looking for, each time THEY decide to buy.

This is a picture of a market that has no liquidity. The presence of day traders and speculators provides a valuable service. They help the market stay liquid, by being a seller or a buyer at many different prices each day. The stock markets do not own the stocks but only facilitate the sell. The stock market allows me to sit in Maui on vacation and buy a stock of a company in Hong Kong from a guy in New York. But it only works if there are sellers when I want to buy and buyers when I want to sell.

Reason Number 3
More Buyers and Sellers create Fair Prices

The presence of the day trader and speculators brings more people to the market to sell and buy and that keeps everyone honest in their pricing. The fact that the company in Hong Kong needed 15 million dollars to expand to South America is not important to me. I am only interested in buying the company's stock at a fair price.

If when I visit E-Trade and ask to buy 100 shares and there were only 2 people selling the stock I was looking for, the scarcity of the stock may cause the price to be higher than its real value. I would then leave the "stock supermarket" to wait or look for the stock when more people were selling and the price would be closer to the fair market value.

Reason Number 4
Businesses Run on Budgets

Grain producers use the Futures Commodity Markets to help with the risks of producing a harvest, only to find that the harvest price is too low to make a profit. Temperature, precipitation and the changing needs of customers all contribute to the supply and demand for commodities like wheat, corn or soybeans. All of these changes affect the price of commodities.

A grain futures contract is a legally binding agreement for the delivery of grain in the future at an agreed-upon price. The contracts are standardized by a futures exchange as to quantity, quality, time and place of delivery. These contracts give another option to farmers to help hedge against bad prices. The speculators again bring more buyers and sellers to the market maintaining fairer prices.

Airline companies that use large amounts of fuel use the fuel futures markets to hedge against the price of oil going up and breaking their budgets.

Finally, the stock markets give savers another investment option. Our Christian value, of being faithful managers of money motivates us to invest our savings in banks, credit unions or individual loans. Not all Christians have the aptitude to run their own business. But they can get the rewards of a growing business by investing in business's shares in the Stock Markets.

In Summary

When people complain about Free Enterprise or capitalism, they never have another system to replace it. Markets will either be free or controlled by someone. Every attempt to control financial markets, beyond Ten Commandment rules has failed to succeed. History has proven that Christian Capitalism is the only system that works consistently and over hundreds of years.

6

The Corrupting Power of Socialism
The Moral Failures of Planned Economies

"There are more instances of the abridgement of the freedom of the people by gradual and silent encroachments of those in power than by violent and sudden usurpations." *James Madison*[19]

In October 2013, the EBT system in a number of Walmarts in Louisiana had a computer problem that caused the system to take the spending limits off all EBT Cards (what was formerly called food stamps.)

Hundreds of people stormed the affected stores and cleared the shelves. EBT card holders began calling their friends. One man was seen with 10 shopping carts stacked high. One store locked its doors, because there were too many people in the store. At 9PM the system started putting the spending limits back on the cards and an announcement was made over the intercom. Within minutes the stores were left with rows of abandoned shopping carts full of perishable items, flat screen TV's, clothes and furniture. Reviewing the contents of the abandoned carts, some shoppers did not even care what they had put in their carts.

The government and private citizen's reactions were mixed. Many felt the pillaging of Walmart was just normal human behavior. We should have assumed that people would hoard food with the EBT system experiencing problems. One man said, "Walmart was lucky there wasn't a riot."

National news organization's cameras broadcast row after row of empty shelves and the now abandoned shopping carts; a visual testimony of the immorality of EBT card holders. Had these people

---

[19] https://www.goodreads.com/author/quotes/63859.James_Madison

always been thieves? Had those who plundered Walmart that day had a sense of right and wrong at one time? What happened to their conscience? Were they taught by their parents that if you can get something for nothing, even if it is stealing, go for it?

Regularly getting free stuff; stuff that you did not work for; stuff that you did not earn corrupts the mind and will. Instead of a safety net of items needed to survive, government charity is no longer viewed as charity by the recipient. There is a right way and a wrong way to help those in need. God's way is described in Chapter 12 of this book. God's way has safeguards to the corrupting power of the 2016 Safety Net. Here are 7 ways that socialistic policies are moral failures.

I. Men Are Encouraged to Covet

Robin Hood Was Right
More $ for the ~~Rich~~ POOR
Hungry? Eat a Banker

The above *Occupy Wall Street* sign was topped by one young woman who penned all her concerns on one single sign. She sat proudly being photographed, for the national media.

Close Corporate Tax Loopholes,
Tax Religious Groups, End The Wars, Legalize Weed,
And Bring Back ARRESTED DEVELOPMENT.

The spirit of covetousness has slowly gained access to Christian's thinking as it gained a place of authority in the United States. Timid and confused religious leaders remain silent, afraid of being called insensitive to the poor.

"A nation will not survive morally or economically when so few have so much while so many have so little..."[20]

This quote from presidential candidate Bernie Sanders is a part of the politics of covetousness. Atheist Karl Marx couldn't have said it better.

---

[20] http://thelibertarianrepublic.com/top-five-dumbest-quotes-from-socialist-presidential-candidate-bernie-sanders

Whenever you hear someone complaining about wage inequality, the speaker is trying to get you to envy how much someone else has and compare it to how much you don't have. This is the actual definition of coveting. As Christians we should take our moral compass from the Ten Commandments; God's view of what is right and what is wrong. Sorry Bernie, sorry Karl, God knows what is best for the human heart.

> 'You shall not covet your neighbor's wife, and you shall not desire your neighbor's house, his field or his male servant or his female servant, his ox or his donkey or anything that belongs to your neighbor.' *Deuteronomy 5:21 NASB*

Ask yourself, "Why does it matter that someone has more than I do?" It does not matter whether your neighbor was given a house or worked for his house or inherited his house. It is his house. Why do you think you deserve a house of equal or greater value?

All political positions that use inequality to gain power begin by comparing one person's circumstances to another's. This comparing opens the door to many problems. It is the opposite of loving your fellow man; even loving the rich man.

The Entitled and Thankfulness

The distorted view of the anti-capitalist goes something like this. "The rich feel entitled. The rich don't feel like the rules apply to them." This idea that the rich feel entitled is the opposite of the truth. The rich usually feel they are only entitled to what they pay for. Of course there are rich and poor men who feel the rules don't apply to them.

But there are as many men who believe that business should be moral, as Charles G. Koch states in his book *Good Profit: How Creating Value for Others Built One of the World's Most Successful Companies.* Because free markets bring accountability much faster than any other system; and because free markets don't favor some men over others; free markets produce more moral rich men than any other system.

The truth is that socialism produces more entitled and unthankful people than capitalism. This is a rational conclusion that can be backed up with studies. If you give men things they have not worked for and then you tell them it is their RIGHT to have the free stuff, you produce men who feel entitled. A RIGHT by definition does not have to be earned. It is given either by God or government.

In socialism you are taught that everyone is entitled to free support. So instead of a few immoral rich people feeling they are entitled, everyone is told they are entitled; entitled because they have a right to the free stuff; and if it is their right there is no reason to be thankful. Instead of fearing rich men, we should fear the entitled and unthankful masses.

To increase socialism men's hearts have to become more immoral. They must be taught to take charity without thankfulness. The government, instead of guarding men's right to "Life, liberty and the pursuit of happiness," guards men's right to free stuff.

II. Immoral Men Get Rich While Hurting the Poor

Those who love big government usually express their concern that the very, very rich are not wise enough or good enough to control so much money. They fear the Koch brothers (but not George Soros – hum?)

I fully agree that rich men are not necessarily wise, moral or even good. There are good and decent men who are among the super-rich. There are corrupt and evil men who are among the super-rich. Those who have this fear of powerful men (usually from the other political party) never explain the following inconsistency.

If men are not "good" enough; or if men cannot be trusted with large sums of money, why would we trust other men with even larger sums of money? George Soros, the Koch Brothers or Warren Buffet does not have the cash flow of the Federal Government. The people's money, when in the hands of the government is no longer the people's money. So why would we give more money to the men of government?

Who are these government men who are so much more moral and wise? What is it about the government bureaucrat or politician that we trust more than the rich man? Is he wiser? Is he more knowledgeable?

It is this 1% of the 1% that gets richer and richer when the government controls and regulates more. This has been evident in the United States.

> "… the biggest wealth gap right now… is between those at the bottom and middle of the 1 percent, and the top .01 percent." …The top 1 percent has grown about 4% a year since the 2000's. "But the top one-hundredth of 1 percent has seen its wealth grow twice that amount. [21]

In 2014, Carlos Slim Helú bumped Bill Gates of Microsoft from his perch as the world's richest man. [22] But Bill Gates took the title back in 2015 according to Forbes.com. It is not as important where the richest rank in their rolls. But it is important how and why they are the richest. Does socialism protect us against men acquiring a lot of money?

The deceptive axiom, *The rich get richer and the poor get poorer* was disproved in the last chapter. But those who feel capitalism is unfair never ask what happens under democratic socialism, when the markets are heavily distorted. Do the rich in socialism get richer? The answer is - drum beat please – in socialism the rich get really, really rich and do it without the headaches of providing competing products or services.

Who Are The 1% of the 1%

1. The Entrepreneur – they start companies that disrupt an existing market or create new markets. We are living in a unique time of history similar to the industrial revolution. There are great opportunities in this area of wealth creation and almost all of these rich are from free market economies.

2. Capitalists with multigenerational wealth who guard their investments from risk and maintain businesses that serves the public.

---

[21] The New York Observer, Nov. 23, 2015; *The Rich List* page 41
[22] forbes.com/ July 15, 2014 *Mexico's Carlos Slim Reclaims World's Richest Man Title From Bill Gates*

3. Businessman in partnership with government controlled markets, almost exclusively in socialistic or other totalitarian countries.

The richest man in 2014, Carlos Slim Helú falls into category #3.

> [He] oversees a vast business empire that is influential in every sector of the Mexican economy and accounts for 40% of the listings on the Mexican Stock Exchange…
>
> The conglomerate comprises a diverse portfolio of businesses from a wide array of industries that include telecommunications, education, health care, industrial manufacturing, food and beverages, real estate, airlines, media, mining, oil, hospitality, entertainment, technology, retail, sports and financial services. [23]

There are men like Carlos Slim Helu who are made very, very rich in every central controlled economy. We do not know whether he is a good man or a bad man. But it is obvious that the Mexican poor would be better off without his businesses having a monopoly by Mexican Government dictate.

With more competition, there would be more business activity and with more activity, there would be more jobs. He has truly become the richest man in the world on the backs of the Mexican poor. All thanks to Socialism, Mexican style.

The rich men who have made their fortunes by crony capitalism made possible by government regulating and restricting markets, are truly unchecked, unmonitored and unaccountable. Where the first two categories of the super-rich answer to the free markets and may be reined in by monopoly laws, the rich businessmen of oppressive governments answer to no-one. Those who fear the Super-Rich's power should fight for free markets and stop socialism's dark atmosphere where evil can grow unchecked.

---

[23] wikipedia.org *Carlos Slim*

III. Men Become Less Generous

The facts about who are the most generous in the world are clear. A professor of business and government policy at Syracuse University, Arthur C. Brooks did an extensive study which became a book titled *Who Really Cares?*

> [W]hen we correct for average income… Even accounting for differences in standard of living, Americans give more than twice as high a percentage of their incomes to charity as the Dutch, almost three times as much as the French, more than five times as much as the Germans, and more than ten times as much as the Italians.

> Americans give at much higher levels and rates than people in practically any other part of the world—not just Western Europe. When we consider other nations, America looks better and better, but Western Europe looks worse and worse: In 1995, Tanzanians gave a larger part of their incomes than Norwegians. Kenyans gave more than Austrians and Germans. And almost everybody—Africans, South Americans, Eastern Europeans—gave more than Italians.[24]

There seems to be two underlying principles which determine whether people are generous in their giving of time, money, and other resources to those who are less fortunate.

1. Is the person Christian or religious?
2. Is the person living in a more conservative or free enterprise culture?

The Democratic Socialists of the world try to take the high ground morally, but are less generous and more concerned with their own well-being than others well-being. This is a fact.

---

[24] Brooks, Arthur C. (2007-12-04). Who Really Cares: The Surprising Truth About Compassionate Conservatism -- America's Charity Divide--Who Gives, Who Do (pp. 120-121). Basic Books. Kindle Edition

In 1835, Alexis de Tocqueville wrote "The Americans make associations to give entertainments, to found seminaries, to build inns, to construct churches, to diffuse books, to send missionaries to the antipodes; in this manner they found hospitals, prisons, and schools." [25]

If Christians in America allow the same spirit of self-centeredness that European Democratic Socialists have, we may see our country lose another Christian value, generosity. If we allow our Government to corrupt human hearts, Americans could grow in echoing the mantra of Democratic Socialists, "Let the government do it."

Instead of humans helping humans, there develops a cold-hearted; one size fits all; get in line government program that is so disconnected from the actual problem that everyone becomes frustrated, discouraged and rebellious. This disconnect is so wide that the bureaucrat asks for more pay than a comparable job in the private sector. Since he elects his boss, it is easy to get a raise for doing substandard work.

And who MORALLY loses out? Everyone: the bureaucrat because he is being paid higher than the fair market value of his job; the citizen who no longer gives as much to charity; the poor who receive substandard service and become less thankful for the charity they receive.

IV. Propaganda, Deception and Hidden Agendas
A Brave New World

Instead of Al Gore's video on Global Warming, all American schools should make *Brave New World* mandatory reading. Much of what Aldous Huxley imagined in 1932 could become our reality. Institutional deception is an important part of controlling citizens as government takes their freedom. Since government programs have no way to measure their success; and since most bureaucrats need to justify next year's budget; success is always just beyond the horizon.

---

[25] Alexis de Tocqueville, Democracy in America, ed. J. P. Maier, trans. George Lawrence

But after decades of failure how do the politicians and their minions justify their failure? They lie.

In free markets, the amount of money that is earned, invested and guarded from risky ventures determines whether you are a success. The wealth created by the product or service being sold is a measure of whether customers are happy. Public opinion is very important to the capitalist. But when tempted to lie about something, he is reined in by the knowledge that customers can leave quickly, when they don't trust him. Citizens have nowhere to go, when they discover the government has lied to them.

American's loss of trust in their government is a clear danger to our Republic. The Pew Research Center in a November 23, 2015 article titled *Beyond Distrust: How Americans View Their Government* show a downward arrow on the graph showing our trust in our government.

> Fewer than three-in-ten Americans have expressed trust in the federal government in every major national poll conducted since July 2007 – the longest period of low trust in government in more than 50 years.[26]

Political PREDICTIONS are now acted upon as if the President is Nostradamus. Here are a few predictions from Earth Day, 1970.

> "Population will inevitably and completely outstrip whatever small increases in food supplies we make. The death rate will increase until at least 100-200 million people per year will be starving to death during the next ten years." *Paul Ehrlich, Stanford University biologist*

> "It is already too late to avoid mass starvation." *Denis Hayes, chief organizer for Earth Day*

> "Scientists have solid experimental and theoretical evidence to support...the following predictions: In a decade, urban dwellers will have to wear gas masks to survive air pollution...by 1985 air

---

[26] http://www.people-press.org/2015/11/23/1-trust-in-government-1958-2015/

pollution will have reduced the amount of sunlight reaching earth by one half...." *Life Magazine, January 1970*

"Dr. S. Dillon Ripley, secretary of the Smithsonian Institute, believes that in 25 years, somewhere between 75 and 80 percent of all the species of living animals will be extinct." *Sen. Gaylord Nelson*

"The world has been chilling sharply for about twenty years. If present trends continue, the world will be about four degrees colder for the global mean temperature in 1990, but eleven degrees colder in the year 2000. This is about twice what it would take to put us into an ice age." *Kenneth Watt, Ecologist*[27]

Why would so many Christians believe the false prophets of our day? The Earth Day predictions continue each year by scientists and politicians who have replaced the man on the street holding the sign, "THE END IS NEAR."

What to Do With the Dissenters

In the *Brave New World*, there were people who would not go along with the program. Christians use to be some of the strongest dissenters against centralized government controls. Now the false prophets have a three pronged attack against dissenters.

1. The dissenters need re-education. They need to do a better job at communicating the truth of their positions to the populace. This is President Obama's default position.

"The debate [on climate change] is over. Climate change is real." Those were Senator Bernie Sander's words at the Democratic debates. It's science and scientists are our new prophets. It is settled.

2. The second bully move to keep the Brave New World progressing is to indignantly insist that Christians are free to practice their religion as long as it is not in the public square. That could offend someone.

---

[27] http://www.ihatethemedia.com/earth-day-predictions-of-1970-the-reason-you-should-not-believe-earth-day-predictions-of-2009

3. The final bully move to silence the dissenters is to laugh or shout them down. Since todays prophets have the same record of accuracy as their 1970's counterparts, they simply don't respond to the argument. The dissenter's arguments are just too absurd to warrant a response.

The answer to this dilemma is for Christians to return to the public square. The issues of honesty, uncovering hidden agendas, exposing businessmen who are making money from government programs, should be thoughtfully addressed. Morality should be defined from the pulpit again. The answer is for the church to wake up and take their responsibilities of self-rule seriously again.

V. Self-Centered Materialism Hurts Others

Socialists act as if people are selfish, because they have more stuff to be selfish about. The poor aren't selfish, only the rich. The Christian's perspective is that every human being is self-centered. We are NOT taught to be sinful. We are born selfish.

Materialism that many associate with capitalism is actually much more of a problem in socialism. Since all men are born self-centered, the poverty and lack of opportunity that controlled economies create ignite even more materialism. Then add the government's message that more stuff is the answer to most problems and you create a self-centered electorate. Finally, exclude religion from the public discourse and materialism becomes the default value system.

Men are also selfish in capitalism. The difference is that free markets teach those who are selfish valuable economic lessons. These lessons do not hurt others and can motivate the selfish person to change their ways. How blessed a nation is, if its financial markets motivate all men to good behavior. It is these good ACTIONS that a Christian should cheer on.

Let us use Milton Friedman's famous PENCIL from his book *Free to Choose*. If a selfish pencil manufacturer is selfish and wants to hurt his competitors, he can underprice his pencils. The lower prices help the public, since people save money buying the cheaper pencils.

The Corrupting Power of Socialism

If the selfish factory owner tries to cut his costs by using cheaper materials, the public will have more choices. His competitors may be helped by taking his customers as they decide they don't like inferior pencils.

No matter what the selfish factory owner does to the pencil market, the public is insulated from the consequences of his actions. His heart can be selfish, but with free markets the product that has value and is priced right benefits everyone needing the product. Everyone is free to enjoy the benefits of free market products and services, no matter what the motives of those in the markets.

It may seem counterintuitive, but the system that provides the most freedom of action, also produces good acts that Christians want to encourage everyone to follow.

It is not counterintuitive to understand how socialism makes men less productive. When opportunities are limited, there is a much larger chance that you will never discover what you do well. Mark Zuckerberg, creator of Face Book lived in an environment that provided enough opportunity to experiment, fail and try again; the more freedom the more opportunities. The more choices a person has; the more chances a person may find what they are good at doing. This is what our country's founders called the "pursuit of happiness."

It is also not counterintuitive to realize that if you allow everyone to be rewarded for their actions; you get more people working to earn those rewards. Men work harder and longer when rewarded fairly. The fairness of this dynamic makes God happy too. Many Gurus are telling young people to try different jobs and find what they like. They never mention that socialism will make this impossible as it limits young people's opportunities.

Self-centered materialism and the seeking of pleasure is the default position of the Democratic Socialists. Capitalism provides the freedom to pursue happiness, by finding a purpose in work, because of the varying opportunities of Free Enterprise.

Don't Worry About Production Rates

While in the Philippines, in 1993 I watched a group of 50 men with wheelbarrows pour cement for a multistory building's foundation. Each man would walk hundreds of feet over flimsy boards with the small wheel barrel filled with concrete and dump it into a large hole. Day after day, I watched as 50 men dumped one wheelbarrow of concrete at a time in the large hole. I left before they were done.

Even now you will hear these central planners lamenting about how they need to "create" more jobs. But as Philippine Markets became more free those 50 men lost their jobs. One man and a concrete truck did what they did in 100th of the time. When you hear government bureaucrats complaining about bad corporations downsizing, remember their answer is to buy more wheelbarrows.

VI. Robbing Men of Hope & Dignity

When I was 23 years old, I lost my job at Western Electric. My unemployment checks came each month and there was no financial reason for me to go back to work. My wife and I were newly married and she was still working. But my pastor called me in to talk with me about going back to work.

He loved me enough to get me doing something, even if it was working for minimum wage. He was wise enough to understand that a 23 year old man should be working, for his own good. I found a job in one week paying more than minimum wage. I didn't stay at this job, but used this 2nd job to buy a house one year later.

My wife's parents and my parents were not financially able to help, and my wife and I never asked. We lived from paycheck to paycheck, as we started our family. Those years helped us become faithful financial stewards. We always ran out of money, before the next paycheck. We budgeted and I began a log book to track our payments, so the lights would not be turned off. Those years when we had nothing and lived on less made us who we are today.

We learned how to overcome fear when we had an unexpected bill.
We learned to budget and have patience when the budget was broken.
We learned how to be happy with few material comforts.
We learned to be thankful for the little things we had.
We learned that we could survive on our own.
We learned to pray, discuss and make hard decisions about money.

We learned patience, courage, wisdom, and generosity toward others, because we lived without – not because we had money. We learned to depend upon ourselves and trust a good God.

It is these character building experiences that the Democratic Socialists rob from their children. It is no wonder that after several generations Socialists panic when it looks like they may have to depend upon themselves. The 2015 riots in Greece showed a fearful people; people who had been robbed of life's valuable lessons of self-reliance.

Because we had no one to help us; no government agency, no rich relative, no church charity; we learned what really is important. We learned that money is NOT the most important thing in life, because we lived without money. We learned the value of money and the how unimportant it is for our real happiness.

Now when I have to pay an expected $20,000 bill or have a client quit that provided hundreds of thousands of dollars in profit to our business, I pray. I don't panic. It is just money.

Avoiding Materialism
… the Roman poet Persius said, "Oh, what void there is in things." Social scientists have repeatedly proven Persius right. In 2011, a group of psychologists at several American universities found that kids who were most attached to material objects were the least grateful for the blessings in their lives, most envious of others, and enjoyed their activities outside of school least. Materialistic kids are unhappy kids.[28]

---

[28] Brooks, Arthur C. (2012-05-08). The Road to Freedom: How to Win the Fight for Free Enterprise (pp. 28-29). Basic Books. Kindle Edition

Money as savior and comforter is found in all economies. The Socialist goes one step further. He elevates money as THE answer. He says we will be happier, if we have more money. The Socialist promotes materialism. The Capitalist can easily fall into the same deception of materialism. But because he is free to gain wealth, earn more money and make financial choices, the deception of materialism is unmasked. Money, security or comfort does not bring happiness, as the Socialist teaches. So what does?

The Satisfaction of Earning Money

The human being has a fairness meter built into his mind. It is often broken, easily deceived and many times ignored. But we know when we have earned something. And we know when we have not earned something. It is this fairness meter that brings us happiness. The Socialist talks about fairness as something that is felt but not easily identified. But we really do know the difference between a gift and something that we have earned.

Arthur Brooks, in his book *The Road to Freedom* points out that it is not money that we really desire, but the earned success that the money symbolizes. When a man works toward a goal and achieves something, he has EARNED whatever the profits are.[29]

As Christians, our goals are first spiritual and second physical. But the fact that our number one pursuit is to achieve spiritual success does not cancel our need to accomplish goals in the physical world. Men who do not work for the money they receive have a fairness meter that must be recalibrated (perverted) by the Socialist.

As Christians, we are concerned that men have sensitive consciences. We are concerned that men know right from wrong and treat one another accordingly. When men do not earn their way, they should be uncomfortable. When men do not earn their way, they should want to work harder – it is only fair. Why is getting regular unearned support fairer?

---

[29] Brooks, Arthur C. (2012-05-08). The Road to Freedom: How to Win the Fight for Free Enterprise (p. 24). Basic Books. Kindle Edition.

VII. No Innovation
Who Will Cure Cancer?

Corporations and private enterprises continually invest in future Research and Development. Most investments are a gamble. But For-Profit companies make money solving a problem or providing a new product or service. So business by definition is continually and without compulsion spending money to solve people's problems. When they are successful, they create jobs and more opportunity for those whom they have helped. The benefit of this investing and creating spirals out and touches more and more people as new products or services develop.

Centralized governments have twisted our language and now call spending money on a problem as investing in the future. Education and fixing the roads are necessary, but they are not doing Research and Development. Government will never find the cure for cancer. Here are the facts about how business is striving to help everyone.

Drug Companies R&D

One hundred drug companies were studied to find out their average R&D cost for 220 new drugs. The average is one billion dollars per drug. That is 220 billion dollars in the last 10 years. [30]

Google, Microsoft, Intel & Samsung

In the list of the top ten companies spending the most on R&D in 2013 are; Samsung $13.4 billion; Intel $10.6 billion; Microsoft 10.4 billion; and Google $8 billion.

The Global Innovation 1000, a list of public companies that spend the most on innovation in 2013 invested a record $647 billion. This was an increase of $9 billion over 2012. [31]

The Bill and Melinda Gates Foundation is the largest private foundation in the world. As of 2013 the Gates had donated 28 billion dollars. [32]

---

[30] Forbes.com *How Much Does Pharmaceutical Innovation Cost?*
[31] Fortune.com *The 10 biggest R&D spenders worldwide*
[32] https://en.wikipedia.org/wiki/Bill_%26_Melinda_Gates_Foundation

Warren Buffet & The Pledge

Warren Buffet, the most successful business investor of the 20th Century created the Giving Pledge with Bill Gates the founder of Microsoft. The pledge is a moral pledge that is directed to billionaires to give away the majority of their assets to do works of philanthropy.

As of 2015, 137 billionaires from 14 countries have signed the pledge. "When we started the Giving Pledge a few years ago, we had no idea we'd get this many people to come together," Bill Gates said in a press release. [33]

The signers of the pledge do not claim any religious affiliation or belief in God. Instead they site two concepts over and over.
1. They had parents who gave and were taught to give as children.
2. They want to give back and want to make the world a better place.

Corporate Philanthropy

Although corporations only gave 5% of the total 2013 charitable giving in the United States, they still gave huge amounts of money to help with society's problems. This level of giving is never seen in Democratic Socialist States. As government takes more, there is less wealth to give to the needy. Here are the top five, by percentage of 2013 pretax profit, as reported by the New York Observer.[34]

#1 Merck $1.86 billion – 33.5% of pretax profit
#2 Pfizer $3.05 billion – 19.4% of pretax profit
#3 Prudential Financial Inc. $71.3 million – 8.9% of pretax profit
#4 Johnson & Johnson $992.6 million – 6.4% of pretax profit
#5 Goldman Sachs Group $262.6 million – 2.2% of pretax profit

Religious Charities

Regular church attenders give more money by percentage of income and by percentage of total giving. I have not detailed the many and varying religious charities that work to help the poor and find cures to

---

[33] http://money.cnn.com/2015/06/02/news/companies/giving-pledge-billionaires-buffett-gates/
[34] New York Observer, The Big Ten, November 2, 2015 page 44-45

our world's problems, in this book. Many former Christian endeavors are now viewed as secular, such as *Habitat For Humanity*. Christians and other religious groups are the largest group of charitable givers in the United States. They reached a record $358.4 billion in 2014.[35]

Capitalism produces the excess wealth that allows individuals to try to solve the problems of our world. Without free markets, our world would have little of the innovations that solve today's problems. As anyone can see, communism and socialism produces little interest in innovating and improving everyone's lives. They are mainly concerned with maintaining control and maintaining an equal substandard living standard for everyone except the rulers.

In Summary

Christians should fight against the corruption of socialism. There are other examples of the corrupting power of economic power centralized into a few hands, beyond the seven listed in this chapter. If you clear your head, of the hundreds of distorted views of men and money, you may find a few more. Email them to me. I would love to consider them as an Appendix II in the next printing of this book.

[35] http://www.csmonitor.com/Business/2015/0616/Charitable-giving-sets-new-record-but-why-are-religious-donations-waning

7

The Christian and Business
Is Business Bad?

When I was 18 years old and working my first job; one of those jobs that you do until you do something else; I had to help the owner of several factories. As we drove to downtown Los Angeles, this successful businessman asked me a simple question. "What do you want to do for a career?"

My answer spoke more about the 1970 educational system's values than what I would eventually do. I answered, "Maybe I will go back to school and become a scientist."

Then he asked me a question that I had never been asked in my short 18 years, "Why not be a businessman?" He seemed to genuinely what to know why business was not one of the things that I had considered. At that time, I did not know why I had never considered business, as a career choice. My father had provided for our family as a successful small businessman and we had all worked in The Dry Cleaners.

I now know why the question seemed so strange to me. In church and at school, business was seen as at best a lower calling and at worst a selfish calling. Television and the movies had taught me the evils of business. Greedy immoral businessmen tried to get as much as they could, while the good guys fought them. This anti-business slant is worse today than it was in the 1960's.

The church's teachings did not help me have a wise or informed view of economics either. I had heard the following ideas in church.
America is too commercialized.
People spend too much money at Christmas.
People spend too much money at Halloween.
Americans buy too much.
People think about material things too much.

Sincere pastors and Christian lay leaders rail against commercialism. In America, capitalism is an easy target. Hearing the anti-commercialism sermons, you would have to conclude that church leadership is anti-business.

It is a small jump from anti-commercialism to anti-capitalism; and then an even easier jump from anti-capitalism to anti-business. The final shift in thinking aligns the church's beliefs with the atheists named in the next chapter. Anti-business totalitarian political thinking is now interwoven into Christian political positions.

Is it no wonder that on Pope Francis' visit to the United States, a Catholic spokesman told Fox News that the Pope was only promoting "Good Communism." How could a Christian nation, so in love with freedom of the individual's right to choose become a society which regulates most buying and selling? It no longer takes a big imagination to see America institute totalitarian financial controls on most businesses.

Budgeting money, credit card spending, good stewardship are all great subjects to teach from the pulpit. When talking about money, the church teaches tithing, giving of alms to the poor, and generous giving from self-sacrifice. The same churches should teach on the goodness of the system that has allowed so much wealth to be accumulated, by so many, The Free Enterprise System.

Jesus and Business Stewardship

... Jesus told them a story because he was near Jerusalem and they thought God's kingdom would appear immediately. He said: "A very important man went to a country far away to be made a king and then to return home. So he called ten of his servants and gave a coin *("mina" three months' pay)* to each servant. He said, 'Do business with this money until I get back...' When he returned home, he said, 'Call those servants who have my money so I can know how much they earned with it.' "The first servant came and said, 'Sir, I earned ten coins with the one you gave me.' The king said to the servant,

'Excellent! You are a good servant. Since I can trust you with small things, I will let you rule over ten of my cities.'
"The second servant said, 'Sir, I earned five coins with your one.' The king said to this servant, 'You can rule over five cities.'

"Then another servant came in and said to the king, 'Sir, here is your coin which I wrapped in a piece of cloth and hid. I was afraid of you, because you are a hard man…

Then the king said to the servant, 'I will condemn you by your own words, you evil servant. You knew that I am a hard man, taking money that I didn't earn and gathering food that I didn't plant.

Why then didn't you put my money in the bank? Then when I came back, my money would have earned some interest.' "The king said to the men who were standing by, 'Take the coin away from this servant and give it to the servant who earned ten coins.' *Luke 19:11-13, 15-21a, 23-24 NCV*

This story is told immediately following Jesus encounter with a very rich businessman, Zacchaeus. Those around Jesus did not like the fact that Jesus was in a rich man's house. It would have been a great time for Jesus to condemn evil capitalistic businessmen.

In this passage, Jesus uses business, investment and profits as His illustrations of good and bad faithfulness. In verse 22, Jesus calls the servant who moved in fear and did not participate in business as an "evil servant." Jesus uses the business world as a good illustration of being a good steward.

The conclusion of this story is only understood in the context of business. At first glance it would seem unfair to take from the poorest man and give to the richest. What is Jesus thinking? But in a business setting (instead of a charity setting) wisdom requires that the best steward is given the most responsibility. In business, this means the most money.

Quaker Business Ethics

From the beginning, Quakers brought new standards of truth and honesty to the conduct of business, putting into practice the testimony of integrity and truth. People realized they could trust Quakers with their money and in the 18th century this led to the rapid growth of Quaker banks such as Barclays and Lloyds.... They also regulated the master-servant and employer-employee relationships in the interest of equality and fairness. People who fell short of these standards were disowned if they did not change their ways.[36]

As free markets evolved in the 19th Century, the Quakers brought their Christian values to their businesses. Quaker businesses grew and were viewed as great successes. Clark's Shoes, Cadbury Chocolate and Western Union became trusted brands. As Christian businesses became more and more profitable they improved the living conditions of their employees. Philanthropy and antislavery campaigns were financed from these same businessmen.

Free Markets Give Christians an Edge

Christians have an edge in free markets.
1. Christians do not lie. They respect contracts and agreements.
2. Christians should be good stewards of other people's assets.
3. Christians strive to be good managers of their own assets.
4. Christians do not want to get rich quick.
5. Christians do not want something for nothing.
6. Christians will not twist the rules to gain an advantage.
7. Christians treat their employees with respect.
8. Christians do not show partiality, but treat people fairly.
9. Christians handle pressure better because they keep the right perspective about money and failure.
10. Christians see their lives as having purpose beyond today.
11. Christians see their actions as being seen by God and they will ultimately be judged by a good, loving but also just God.
12. Christians have a good work ethic. Success in business requires harder work than most jobs.

---

[36] http://www.quakersintheworld.org/quakers-in-action/39

You may be able to think of several other character values that make serious Bible believing Christians valuable in the business world. The families that have the most disposal income in any community are the successful business owners. It would be nice to have this excess cash flow in Christian's hands.

Government Regulations vs Christian Conscience

Government regulations can only catch a few businesses that are cheating. But free markets that have a large percentage of Christian businesses will crowd the fraudulent businesses out of the markets, by keeping their trusting clients happy.

Sermons on greed, over-consumption and how much Americans spend on pet food can be easily viewed as anti-capitalist. These anti-business attitudes have left the businesses of America in the hands of unbelievers and anti-God forces. There are thousands of inspiring stories about God's values working in the business world. Have you heard any lately in church?

Legitimate Christian businessmen spend long hours during the week working in hostile atmospheres, only to find no encouragement on Sunday morning. There is one group of people who are seldom ministered to on Sunday morning – For-profit businessman.

NOW is the time for all Christian communities to stand together. Here are few initiatives that every church could begin.

1. Identify the Christians in the business community of your city.
2. Encourage those in business with solid Bible principles of faith, love and hope.
3. Stop generalized negative comments about commercialism, evil businesses or the American Dream.
4. Stop generalized negative comments about For-profit businesses and overpaid CEO's or sarcastic comments about profits.
5. Teach inspirational businessman stories of God winning by providing answers and serving others.
6. Stop talking negatively about capitalism and free markets.
7. Stop talking as if a "calling" in business is lessor than any other calling.

The Christian and Business

The Church Group as a Market

Every church is a special marketplace, much different from the secular marketplaces. Small, medium and large churches have well connected groups of trusting people who have a heart to help those in their church. Most of these people also could use a separate stream of income.

As much as I am pro-business on Sunday morning and every other day of the week, I am against businesses using kind and sometimes foolish church groups to make profit. Church leaders have a responsibility to protect the "sheep" from wolves. When the church meets, no one should wonder about people's motives; especially leader's motives.

Multi-level marketing, questionable products, services marked up 1000 times, home party products all use unsuspecting church members. The get *Get Rich Quick* message touts large profits with little work. It is a free country and we are free to do what we want, but leaders are free to watch over their sheep and protect from questionable business opportunities. Sadly many of these questionable multilevel marketing schemes are promoted by church leaders, or their families.

As pastor, I taught two things from the pulpit. God wants Christians in business and God doesn't want us taking advantage of our church relationships to make money. As pastor, I had a business that grossed over one million dollars a year, and none of that money came from my relationships in the church. The sheep could always trust that I was there for them, with no hidden agenda to make money.

Christian Businesses or Good Service

There has been a hope that "Kingdom" businesses could be supported by church members. And I am not opposed to Christian businessmen working together and supporting one another. Christian business referral websites and church business bulletin boards are good tools for marketing Christian businesses. But I do not think that bad or over priced products should be supported just because they are being sold by Kingdom Businesses. We may be sheep, but we should be smart sheep.

Free markets work the best when people allow righteous principles to weed out the bad businesses. Buying insurance from your friend at church and then getting an inferior product is unrighteous. Businesses that market only to the Christian community may not be doing a good job for their clients. I hired a management company that was promoted by a widely known ministry and after two weeks of really, really bad service terminated our relationship. I imagine that there was no motivation to provide even mediocre service due to the closed market of clients that came from church promotion.

As a young pastor, I invested $10,000 with a Christian businessman that assured me that his investment was legit. Five years later he was serving a five year prison term and the investment firm sent me a $600.00 settlement check. I trusted this man, because a spiritual father trusted him. Millions of dollars were lost to the church by this one dishonest person marketing to the trusting "sheep." Leaders need to be discerning – Christians are called sheep for a reason.

Encouraging Those Skilled In Business

Just because you *want to be your own boss*, or you *have a great idea to make a million dollars*, this does not mean you should go into business. God can give men favor, blessings, and encouragement, but the skill set to succeed in business is not something everyone has. Not everyone can handle the pressures and the challenges.

Leaders should ask those successful in business and wanting to serve in church to give counsel to those thinking about starting a business. It is these men and women who should be helping those seeking guidance. Everyone who is successful in business has been discouraged to even try. These opinions to "Play it Safe" stop many from even starting. Pulpit ministry should view anti-business comments as seeds sown into the hearts of men.

Let us start sowing seeds of faith that God will bless us with success in business. Let us love and support all those who work hard; even the business owner. Whether they are rich or poor; working by the hour or salaried, let us bless those who work hard and honor them as valued members of our churches.

8

The Enemies of Capitalism
The Greatest Evils of the 20th Century

What does the following groups all have in common?

Totalitarian Governments
Communist Governments
Socialist Governments
Democratic Socialist Governments
Islamic Terrorists
Secular Humanists
Luddites

The historical enemies of Christianity are also the enemies of Free Enterprise. The same authors, government leaders and political activists have fought capitalism and Christianity. Each group above has its own reasons to fight capitalism but they all want less economic freedom.

Sadly many Evangelical and Mainline Christians are in agreement with these atheists, agnostics, anti-religion educators, and socialist politicians. As these unbiblical concepts have slowly gained acceptance, Christians have incorporated these concepts into their Christian world view.

Why would we Christians be in agreement with our enemies about a subject that so affects all our lives; about a subject that affects our freedom to serve God? Money and how we use it is a moral and spiritual issue. Jesus talked about money and our use of it as much as any subject other than faith.

The doctrines of the enemies of Capitalism are based upon two unbiblical principles.

1. Men are basically good and circumstances make them sin. Thus as we change the circumstances of men, they will evolve into better men through education and other human interactions.

2. There are no absolute truths. The end justifies the means. Unjust acts, bad acts and evil acts are OK, if they accomplish good; good is defined by man, not God.

Without these two foundational lies, the enemies of capitalism could not make their doctrines seem logical. These two truths are interwoven into the reasoning of the enemies of capitalism. They are the opposite of the Bible's views. It is no wonder that the men who birthed these ideas are atheists or anti-church.

The Atheists

Before Marx could write his *The Manifesto of the Communist Party,* the doctrines of the Bible had to be replaced by other doctrines that require just as much faith. These ideas so permeate our culture, including our church culture that we no longer treat them as the radical ideas that they were, when they were first proposed.

Thomas Hobbes - *Leviathan*
The Father of Moral Relativism
Man was not made in God's Image

Thomas Hobbes created an alternate view of primitive man. His idea of mankind was that in our natural state, we have no conscience and do what makes us feel good. Thus we have a right to do whatever we want to do. Hobbes does not add, as most of us do today, "As long as it doesn't hurt anyone else."

Thomas Hobbes, an atheist, created an alternative to the Bible's view of the nature of human beings. Our politicians regularly speak of Hobbes *Natural Man,* when describing why a government program is needed. If there is no ultimate good or bad, by what authority can you tell the public what to do? Benjamin Wiker states the *Leviathan* effect:

... if a society acts according to Hobbes's notion of rights, then it becomes, increasingly, a fractious, rights-demanding, passion-driven collection of self-willed individuals hell-bent on getting whatever they desire no matter the cost, and all the while claiming they have a right to what leads to their own and society's self-destruction.[37]

Democracy becomes Aristotle's BAD Democracy when practiced by Hobbes' *Natural Man.* As Christians we believe that men are created in God's image with the potential and call to a higher mission than self-gratification. We also believe men are selfish and if given the freedom to lie, cheat and steal, they will oppress their fellow man. Yet Christians stand quietly while they are told that if we just give people more of what they want, through the next government program, those same men will be better off for it.

Jean-Jacques Rousseau
Discourse on the Origin and
Foundations of Inequality among Men
There Is No Right or Wrong

Jean-Jacques doctrines of original man as a care-free happy person, thinking only of himself have distorted our society's definition of success. It is the enemies of capitalism who created today's anti-work ethic. Men should be left to do whatever makes him happy. The amount of time that we have to play, fellowship or party is compared to how much time we spend working. Vacation Time, Sick Time, and Paid Family Leave, have become a "right" for all men.

Many of today's political answers to large societal problems come from Jean-Jacques doctrines of men's origin. Sinful man's state (his natural state) was the best he could achieve. All rules, all of society's laws, and all religious restraints have caused us humans to fall from this state of the HAPPY primitive man.

---

[37] Wiker, Benjamin (2008-05-06). 10 Books that Screwed Up the World: And 5 Others That Didn't Help (p. 40)

Not just sexual morality, but all morality was unnatural. For "men in that [primitive] state" were entirely amoral: as they did not have "among themselves any kind of moral relationship or known duties, they could be neither good nor evil, and had neither vices nor virtues."

Morality is therefore purely artificial. It develops only with society. Because society itself is not natural, neither is morality. "Savages are not evil," Rousseau asserts, "precisely because they do not know what it is to be good."[38]

There is not only no sin, but no accountability to a higher authority. If we just let humans be humans there would be no restraints; we would just live free and enjoy ourselves. Society's inequalities should be addressed at the root of the problem, which is the fact that we are not letting men be "natural men."

Governments follow the doctrines of Rousseau, when they force some to give to others, because they "need" more. If a man feels he needs more food, housing, recreation, parks, childcare; the man should be able to take these things from others. Jean-Jacques's unchristian doctrines were the foundation of the 1960's Free Love philosophy that has now morphed into Occupy Wall Street.

Just review the present day competition between the Socialist State of California versus the Socialist State of Hawaii in mandating employee benefits. Upon the assumption that, "who wouldn't want another paid day off," they pass one law after another; helping the primitive man.

The Hobbes-ites & Rousseau-ites

Each of the following individuals laid a stone upon the foundation of today's anti-capitalist view point. Christians should be careful how they align their views with the following crowd.

---

[38] Wiker, Benjamin (2008-05-06). 10 Books that Screwed Up the World: And 5 Others That Didn't Help (p. 47). Regnery Publishing. Kindle Edition.

Charles Darwin in his book *The Descent of Man* laid the foundation for the totalitarian Hitler's Eugenics movement. Here is an excerpt.

> If... various checks . . . do not prevent the reckless, the vicious and otherwise inferior members of society from increasing at a quicker rate than the better class of men, the nation will retrograde, as has occurred too often in the history of the world. We must remember that progress is no invariable rule.[39]

Margaret Sanger, the foundress of Planned Parenthood, also supported Hitler. Her book *The Pivot of Civilization* formed a logical rationale for mass murder. You can get Sanger's vile book from several publishers but not from Planned Parenthood.

Betty Friedan's book *The Feminine Mystique* birthed The Feminist Movement that morphed from wanting women to be treated fairly in the work place into the pro-abortion and pro-partial birth (full term) abortion movements.

> Despite her attempts to hide her radical past, Friedan was not an innocent suburban housewife who suddenly realized she was unrealized. She had been a Marxist since her college days at Smith in the late 1930s and early 1940s. In the years after, she belonged to, worked for, or wrote positively about a string of leftist organizations and publications...[40]

Karl Marx
The Manifesto of the Communist Party
A Godless Utopia Is Possible

U.S.S.R.: 20 million deaths;   China: 65 million deaths;
Vietnam: 1 million deaths;   North Korea: 2 million deaths;
Cambodia: 2 million deaths;   Eastern Europe: 1 million deaths;
Latin America: 150,000;   Africa: 1.7 million deaths;

---

[39] Charles Darwin, The Descent of Man, and Selection in Relation to Sex, Princeton University Press, 1981, Part I, Ch. 5, pg. 177

[40] Wiker, Benjamin (2008-05-06). 10 Books that Screwed Up the World: And 5 Others That Didn't Help (p. 219). Regnery Publishing. Kindle Edition.

Total deaths of communists approaches 100 million people killed. [41]

Karl Marx's revolution was the single most destructive force in the 19th and 20th Centuries. The dream of making life wonderful, for everyone except the rich, didn't quite measure up to the reality. As Christians, we look forward to Heaven on Earth, only when Jesus returns. How has Marxism invaded today's Christianity?

Today, it takes a lot of faith to still believe in the theories of Karl Marx? But this atheist's slightly tweaked theories are still stated with conviction by pastors, professors and other left leaning intellectuals.

The concept that "The Ruling Class is bad and oppresses the Worker Class," is still used to rally the masses to rise up and fight. Fight who? The 1%'ers, the rich, the multi-national corporations...

We Christians have been the enemies of communism throughout the 20th Century. But now that communism has failed everywhere, the same ideas continue in sermons and speeches.

Lenin
Vladimir Ilyich Ulyanov
It is RIGHT to take property

Lenin in search of Marx's Heaven on Earth; and deceived by Hobbes' distortion of man; violently killed capitalists, seized their property and set up a dictatorship of the Proletariat. [42]

One of Lenin's favorite books was *The Prince.* Lenin combined the Godless beliefs of the atheists, Marx and Hobbes with Machiavelli, the author of The Prince. Machiavelli encourages leaders to rule by deception, cruelty and evil. In *The Prince,* the end always justifies the means. Lenin took Machiavelli's ideas to new heights calling evil good and good evil. [43]

---

[41] The Black Book of Communism: Crimes, Terror, Repression by Stephane Courtois
[42] The State and Revolution, in Lenin, Essential Works of Lenin Ch. I, Sec.4, 282
[43] Lenin: A Biography, Robert Service 8-10, 203-204, 376

The Enemies of Capitalism

Lenin's revolution set up a proletarian dictatorship that he called a Democracy. These same ideas of using government to do more and more "good," by exerting more and more power have infected most governments in the 21st Century. Because we call our governments Democracies, we feel free. And we are told by our governments that we are free because we can vote. Instead we should insist upon LIMITED government, period.

Lenin pursued a Godless Utopia and killed six to eight million of his own citizens. Stalin took over from him and murdered another twenty to twenty-five million. His intentions were to achieve what many people still hold as a noble pursuit. Christians should not be deceived by the Godless doctrines of:

> From each according to his ability, to each according to his needs;[44]

> Summarized perfectly by, "Society exists without a state, no one owns anything because everyone owns everything, and all is well for the first time in human history."[45]

Today, the same doctrines of Machiavelli, Hobbes, Lenin, Stalin, and Marx; in association with others who were vowed anti-capitalists are again regularly repeated. Two decades ago, these doctrines were veiled in terms of charity. Now the anti-capitalism crowd has revealed their true values and beliefs. Here are the doctrines of today's anti-rich.

Doctrines of the Present Day Anti-Rich

Unemployment

Men want to work. Rewarding men to not work does not produce more men not working. How dare we say the unemployed are lazy.

Bible: Men can be lazy, irresponsible and sometimes need motivation to work and take care of themselves and others. II Thess. 3:10; Proverbs 6:6, 6-9, 13:4, 19:24; 20:4, 21:25

---

[44] The State and Revolution, in Lenin, Essential Works of Lenin Ch. V Sec 4, 343
[45] 10 Books that Screwed Up the World: And 5 Others That Didn't Help (p. 118).

Success in Business

"If you've got a business — you didn't build that. Somebody else made that happen." *The President of the United States – Barak Obama*

The President's supporters defended him by saying this statement was taken out of context. The President was talking about all the wonderful things the government does for all of us and point to the President saying as he summarized his speech, "The point is … that when we succeed, we succeed because of our individual initiative, but also because we do things together. [46]

The Democratic Party spin machine approached the problem with a pure Machiavelli argument. He didn't convey the right message. What he meant is not as important as what the people heard.

Bible: Business success and the wealth it generates is the property of those who created the service or product. Exodus 20:17, Deut. 5:21

Taxes, Morality and Your Stuff

Democratic candidate for president, Bernie Sanders, does not think that a 90% tax rate is too high. Many other tax and spend liberals have been asked that question for decades. Bernie was honest enough to tell us, while the rest only muttered confusing Machiavellian responses.

Bernie and a large percentage of the Democratic Party are only 10% away from Lenin's view of property ownership. Of course in the United States, the government will not put a literal gun to your head to get its money. They will send the IRS.

> When talking about President Dwight Eisenhower's administration, Sanders said, "I think the highest marginal tax rate was something like 90 percent."
>
> CNBC's John Harwood then said, "It was 90. When you think about 90 percent, you don't think that's obviously too high?"

---

[46] http://www.factcheck.org/2012/07/you-didnt-build-that-uncut-and-unedited/

Sanders replied, "No. What I think we've seen, and what frightens me again, when you have the top one-tenth of 1 percent owning almost as much wealth as the bottom 90 percent. Does anybody think that that is the kind of economy this country should have? Do we think it's moral?[47]

Bible: Morality does not have anything to do with how much money you have, but what you have done with the money. Moral wealth is money earned morally. Ma.25:14-28

Socialized Medicine
"If you like your health plan, you can keep your plan."

Debating how much the government should help poor people get health insurance is beyond the scope of this book. But the process of how Obama Care was sold to the electorate speaks to the Federal Government's Machiavellian ethics; the end justifies the means.

"If you like your health plan, you can keep your health plan," was said so many times by President Obama, that everyone who paid attention can still hear it ringing in their ears. It has now been documented that no one believed this statement to be true. It was simply a lie. I believe that much of what President Obama says, he really believes. But the facts are in on this lie. The political leaders believed it was the right thing to do, to lie to the citizens of the United States.

Politifact.com does fact checks on statements made by today's politicians. President Obama is graded as telling the truth only 21% of the time and being mostly truthful only 27% of the time; that is one out of five times that Obama is telling the whole truth; Machiavellian?

When Christians align their political beliefs with the anti-capitalist atheists, they are disconnected from their own values. They are continuing a deception that propagated the greatest evils of the 20th Century. We should STOP IT.

---

[47] http://www.newsmax.com/Politics/Bernie-Sanders-tax-wealthy-90-percent/2015/05/27/id/647105

9

Revelation & Jesus' Return
End Times Financial Systems

There are many interpretations of the visions of John the Beloved on the Island of Patmos. Whether you approach the book of Revelation as symbolic, literal or poetic, the book can reveal insight into God's view of world systems. Whether you think that the events are in the past; in the present; in the near future; or hundreds of years away; the book describes a time of evil totalitarian rule.

For the purposes of this book, I am only addressing God's view of the governments and financial systems of the book. Here are a few simple observations. I will leave everything else to other authors.

Anarchy - No Control
Republics - Limited Control
Socialist Systems - Heavy Regulation
Totalitarian - No Freedom

One of the ways that governments can be categorized is from *No Government* to *No Freedom*. Once we see what type of governments Revelation calls evil, we can work against those types. We start with the foundational truth that God works against evil. And if God works against evil, we should also work against evil and that includes evil governments.

God Always Dislikes Anarchy
First of all, then, I urge that entreaties *and* prayers, petitions *and* thanksgivings, be made on behalf of all men, for kings and all who are in authority, so that we may lead a tranquil and quiet life in all godliness and dignity. *I Timothy 2:1-2 NASB*

Every person is to be in subjection to the governing authorities. For there is no authority except from God, and those which exist are established by God. *Romans 13:1 NASB*

Anarchy, by definition is the state of having no organized government. But when there is no order, a new order quickly forms. War Lords and evil men create their own order out of the chaos and then steal, kill and destroy. The lack of law allows men to do evil with the only restriction being how big their guns are. The conclusion; we need government.

The Four Horseman of the Apocalypse

When He broke the second seal, I heard the second living creature saying, "Come." And another, a red horse, went out; and to him who sat on it, it was granted to take peace from the earth, and that men would slay one another; and a great sword was given to him.

When He broke the third seal, I heard the third living creature saying, "Come." I looked, and behold, a black horse; and he who sat on it had a pair of scales in his hand. And I heard something like a voice in the center of the four living creatures saying, "A quart of wheat for a denarius, and three quarts of barley for a denarius; and do not damage the oil and the wine." *Revelation 6:3-6 NASB*

World War & Financial Disruptions

The 2nd Horseman brings war and the 3rd Horseman brings unstable, inflated economics and famine. To have a World War, you must have two sides. To those who only see the evil nations described in the book, I would contend that there is a group of evil nations that is fighting another group of nations. I will call this "good" group of nations Resister Nations. We Christian's should align our politics with the Resister Nations, even if the events are hundreds of years in the future.

And the great dragon was thrown down, the serpent of old who is called the devil and Satan, who deceives the whole world; *Revelation 12:9a NASB*

Then I saw a beast coming up out of the sea.... There was given to him a mouth speaking arrogant words and blasphemies, and authority to act for forty-two months was given to him. And he opened his mouth in blasphemies against God, to blaspheme His name and His tabernacle, that is, those who dwell in heaven. It was also given to him to make war with the saints...

Then I saw another beast coming up out of the earth... And he deceives those who dwell on the earth... And he causes all, the small and the great, and the rich and the poor, and the free men and the slaves, to be given a mark on their right hand or on their forehead, and he provides that no one will be able to buy or to sell, except the one who has the mark, either the name of the beast or the number of his name. *Revelation 13:1a,5-7a,11a,14a,16-17 NASB*

Everyone has heard of the *Mark of the Beast.* Since Swedish office workers now have the option to implant an RFID chip in their hands to access security doors, we have come to a time that this scripture can be a literal reality.[48]

But by focusing upon how the *Mark of the Beast* may literally happen, we may miss the main point. There are and will be systems that try to control all buying and selling. By controlling the ability to freely buy and sell, these systems can force their will upon everyone.

In the above passages, we see a World War and evil men trying to take over the world's economy. Full regulations on all buying and selling is instituted; a socialist's dream. If you believe that these passages will literally happen; that evil will try to take over all the world's economies and control all transactions; then you should fight all systems that try to control buying and selling.

If this is only symbolic, we Christians (the saints of Revelation13:7) should be even more vigilant to fight socialism. The meaning of the symbolism seems very clear. It is not a big jump from a heavily controlled socialistic economy to full control of that economy. Greek banks closed in the summer of 2015 stopping most buying and selling in a country that thought they were a Democracy.

---

[48] http://www.bbc.com/news/technology-31042477

It is a much harder thing to control limited government, Ten Commandment based free markets. You must first get the citizens to accept ever increasing controls, regulating their day to day monetary transactions. Whether symbolic or literal, the *Mark of the Beast* should motivate us toward fighting for Free Enterprise.

Unfortunately, we have been taught by government schools for decades that government regulation is good and protects us from the abuses of business. A born again Christian, President George W. Bush banned the buying and selling of incandescent light bulbs; Good Controls?

Many good intentioned Christians do not see the big picture, of the book of Revelation. Evil has a hard time controlling a system that is free. Instead of fearing government regulations, 50% of Americans and most of the rest of the world, view regulations as their salvation.

Politicians now feel that it is their job to protect everyone. The Mayor of New York announced that, "People would be arrested," if they tried to travel in the last snow storm. This dependence upon government protection caused parents in Flint Michigan to allow their children to drink orange water and be poisoned. What a tragedy. Today, it is easy to see how free citizens can be encouraged to receive a "Mark" to buy and sell.

Babylon Has Fallen

After these things I saw another angel coming down from heaven, having great authority, and the earth was illumined with his glory. And he cried out with a mighty voice, saying, "Fallen, fallen is Babylon the great! She has become a dwelling place of demons and a prison of every unclean spirit, and a prison of every unclean and hateful bird.

For all the nations have drunk of the wine of the passion of her immorality, and the kings of the earth have committed *acts of immorality* with her, and the merchants of the earth have become rich by the wealth of her sensuality."

> I heard another voice from heaven, saying, "Come out of her, my people, so that you will not participate in her sins and receive of her plagues... Revelation 18:1-4 NASB

The historic city of Babylon was a totalitarian dictatorship that ruled much of the world. This vision reveals a new city-state having seductive influence and control over nations, businesses and the men who are in positions of authority.

A simplistic and naïve interpretation of Chapter 17 and 18's vision of Babylon is that all business is bad. Look at the evil businessmen of verse three above. They have become wealthy and now in verse four we are called to "Come out of her..."

But this scripture is not warning against being businessmen. As Chapter 7 of this book stated, we Christians are more equipped to be in the business world than those who have a bad moral code. The world needs Christians in the places of influence and authority and that includes the business world.

Described here is an intoxicating (*they have drunk of her wine...*) and immoral relationship between governments and businesses. This union is described as unclean and full of demons. Today, we call this union of secular government with big business as a private-public partnership. Secular non-profits now form a most unholy union with business and government.

The next chapter describes the evil alliances in Haiti that non-profits, several governments and businessmen forged as they tried to make money and rebuild Haiti. The country is no better today than before. Haiti's neighbors have a much higher standard of living. Why?

Today is the day to stand and fight for our economic freedom. It is this decentralized, limited government atmosphere that stops evil men from gaining great influence. Today the battle is raging between men who want free markets and those want to control markets by deception and manipulation.

I am not labeling individual men who believe in socialism, communism, or big bureaucracies "antichrist." There are very good, sincere Christians, who have seen the abuses of perverted crony capitalism, and who want more regulations. They are convinced that taking away men's freedom will make a better society.

But let us be honest. The majority of heavy handed government regulations are made by the same people who are also anti-public expressions of religion; anti-church influence; anti-Israel; anti-religion in their political positions. Sound familiar? Most of those who fight to control the markets have the same spirit described in Revelation as antichrist.

The Only Utopia

Although it is not relevant to this book's subject, I cannot end without summarizing my view of the end of the book of Revelation; the end of the New Testament apostolic writings. The book describes a transition from one age to the next; and what will the New Age look like?

God wins and His love banishes the forces of darkness. Jesus the only truly righteous King and Judge assumes authority over a Kingdom that will have no end. The first thousand years of this kingdom restores the Garden of Eden on earth. What atheist doctrines tried to form without God, God accomplishes.

Jesus as the perfect ruler can righteously rule over a Kingdom that has authority over the whole Earth. But I view the human governments of this time period as still being limited, local and of course, Ten Commandment based.

The whole Earth will be filled with the Glory of God and Heaven will be on Earth; the Garden of Eden not just restored; but a Garden of Eden fulfilling God's original intent; God walking with men as they live their lives in the physical realm.

10

The Death of Free Markets
The Fog of Democratic Socialism

In a Ten Commandment based Democracy there are civil servants. These public servants include the elected and the appointed. As a Democracy loses its Christian values a self-centered electorate votes for more and more free stuff.

> Democracy must be something more
> Than two wolves and a sheep
> Voting on what to have for dinner
> *James Bovard - libertarian author*[49]

Within a BAD Democracy, the public servant changes into a bureaucrat who no longer serves. Instead he has more and more laws to interpret and enforce. The bureaucrat becomes an enforcer; someone who makes sure the public funds are used in a way that HE feels is best. The laws are written in general terms and then given to unelected officials to administer as they see fit.

As the dependent citizen's cries crescendo, "Get something done. Get more done." The citizens who are asking for restraint and a return to conservativism are drowned out.

The public servant's role was first modeled from Christian Servant-Leadership principles. The servant of the public has now become the bureaucratic administrator. He is modeled from the cold, unattached character of a Roman Emperor's administrators.

A system that gives large amounts of authority to unelected individuals is by definition oppressive. The more authority you give these bureaucrats the more oppressive the government becomes.

---

[49] https://en.wikiquote.org/wiki/James_Bovard

The Founding Fathers and Christian Values

Christian values must be the foundation of any democracy. Our founding fathers knew this and stated it countless times. Here are a few of the founding father's statements.

> Only a virtuous people are capable of freedom. As nations become corrupt and vicious, they have more need of masters.

> Whereas true religion and good morals are the only solid foundations of public liberty and happiness . . . it is hereby earnestly recommended to the several States to take the most effectual measures for the encouragement thereof. *Continental Congress, 1778 Benjamin Franklin, Signer of the Declaration of Independence"*

> The moral principles and precepts contained in the scriptures ought to form the basis of all our civil constitutions and laws. . . All the miseries and evils which men suffer from vice, crime, ambition, injustice, oppression, slavery, and war, proceed from their despising or neglecting the precepts contained in the Bible. *Noah Webster, author of the first American Speller and the first Dictionary*

> "We have no government armed with power capable of contending with human passions unbridled by morality and religion . . . Our Constitution was made only for a moral and religious people. It is wholly inadequate to the government of any other." *John Adams, signer of the Declaration of Independence, the Bill of Rights and our second President.* [50]

I do not agree with some of the observations of Alexis de Tocqueville in his book *Democracy in America* (1835/1840), but he did notice that American Democracy was based upon moral principles, not just law.

> Since Americans built their social order from the ground up, their understanding of liberty is quite the opposite of extreme democracy's view of liberty as the freedom to do whatever one

---

[50] http://www.free2pray.info/5founderquotes.html selected quotes

wants. Rather, for Americans, liberty is an achievement, the result of individuals learning to rule themselves; that is, true liberty rests on a solid moral foundation. Liberty is not license, let alone, as modern liberalism would have it, licentiousness. *Tocqueville quotes an excerpt of a speech by one John Winthrop*[51]

As long as the majority keeps being promised more and more stuff, the majority votes for the party of free stuff. As new laws and new regulations are passed and then given to faceless nameless bureaucrats to enforce, free markets are distorted. Each law takes one more freedom away from someone. The politician never answers the question, "How much is enough?"

The Unseen Hand of Soft Tyrants
The Democratic Socialist State of Maui

Our country is now full of small tyrants. City and county governments have jumped upon the regulation bandwagon. In Maui County Hawaii, a relatively small county with 160,000 residents, some citizens may wait 17 years to get a water meter *(for new home development.)*

> The Upcountry water meter priority list has gone from 1,887 properties in 2013, when the list was closed, to 1,765 as of Friday, about a year after the water department began issuing meters to long-waiting applicants. At this rate, it could take as long as 17 years to go through the long list of Upcountry residents who want a meter.[52]

Maui County makes people, who want to build a house wait years. Without water meters they can't get a building permit. Large builders have learned to pay ransom to these small tyrants. Usually *Low Income Housing* is the ransom required to build a new project.

When building the first new church building in Palmdale California in forty years, I had to jump through hundreds of government hoops.

[51] 10 Books Every Conservative Must Read: Plus Four Not to Miss and One Impostor (p. 118). Regnery Publishing. Kindle Edition.
[52] mauinews.com 10/10/2015

The mayor talked with me about how the city needed the services of more churches. But even in this conservative city the bureaucracy was unrestrained. To fight city hall was discouraged.

Hundreds of new Federal regulations overlapped new California regulations; which overlapped new LA County Earthquake regulations. Then the City regulated the color of the building and how much grass HAD to be planted. Ironically, it is now illegal for the mandated sod to be watered by the same city government, due to the draught of 2015.

The City of Palmdale has hundreds of regulations that effect all city visitors and citizens. They control what each citizen plants in their front yard; what color they can paint their house; if they can park their car in front of their house.

The World's 10th Largest Economy
The Cost of Federal Regulation

In my annual report for the Competitive Enterprise Institute titled Ten Thousand Commandments: An Annual Snapshot of the Federal Regulatory State, I calculate that the cost of federal economic, environmental and health and safety regulation is around $1.86 trillion annually, based upon government data.[53]

The above quote from Clyde Wayne Crews Jr. reveals how much of our economy has been taken over by unelected faceless men, writing and then enforcing new regulations. Many of these NEW rules will cost over 100 million dollars each year. Few have a full cost-benefit analysis.

Each rule may be written with the intent to help, protect or encourage proper economic behavior. But we should stop judging regulations on whether they have good intentions. We should fight for laws that would limit the ability of government to regulate, period.

I came home from working a 16 hour day, the day that President Obama signed the Affordable Care Act into law. As I stood in my

---

[53] Forbes magazine June 30, 2014 pg. 40

bedroom at 3AM and watched the President sign the law, I saw with each stroke of his signature invisible bondage, released into our nation.

While all eyes were on Obama Care, the President and Congress passed 217 bills in 2010, a relatively small number. But the regulatory agencies issued 3,573 final rules; 3,573 new strokes of the pen; 3,573 new LAWS; each taking away someone's freedom to act without oversight. [54]

It is this BAD Democracy that has created a web of bondage. BAD Democracy has taken GOOD Republic hostage and we all are like sheep. Do we really need to be regulated this much?

The Hybrid Government / Business Solution

What is called capitalism, in most of the world is a hybrid form of socialist governments and amoral businesses that create an unholy alliance. In the last chapter, I equated these hybrids to Revelation's Whore of Babylon. The businesses become intoxicated with the prospect of great wealth and little competition. They form unholy unions and their goal is to get rich by taking away free choice and competition from the markets.

Businesses in the free markets develop good Learning Curves. But when you couple business, government and charitable foundations there is no such thing as a Learning Curve. The confusion of Babylon is evident when these three entities enter into unholy alliances.

Governments by themselves, rarely develop a Learning Curve from their mistakes. Government, business and non-profits all define success in different ways. Thus failure is defined differently. This three goal approach always forms a fog of confusion. If you disagree with this Babylonian – confused approach, you are accused of not having a heart for whomever the government program is focused upon; a heart for the homeless; a heart for the poor; a heart for the uninsured.

---

[54] 2011 Ten Thousand Commandments, An Annual Snapshot of the Federal Regulatory State page 2

Evil is rewarded faster in an atmosphere of confusion. Problems do not have to be solved in this modern day system of confusion. Problems just need to be addressed and tax dollars spent on them.

Evil Alliances in Haiti

Peter Schweizer's book Clinton Cash describes unrighteous, unchristian "help" that many sincere people attempted to give to the people of Haiti. Peter, in Chapter 10 of Clinton Cash, describes the union between the loosely run government of Haiti, the United States Government (Clinton's State Department), For-profit contractors (with little experience), foreign corporations, non-profit charities and The Clinton Foundation. The sad failure of each endeavor has left the people of Haiti still poor but a few well connected politicians and political cronies much richer.[55]

Winning the Argument for Free Markets

This unique experiment in self-rule, we call the United States is about to be perverted into something that is similar to other much more oppressive systems of rule.

I have spent my life in the Christian community of America. And most of us avoid confrontation and do not like to argue. We prefer to have peace with our neighbor, even if that means just shutting up about politics and religion. By being "nice" people we have given the public forum to those who are the most antichristian.

If we do not decide to stand up and speak, the anti-Israel, antichristian and antichrist crowd will increase in their influence. With little resistance, they bully the public discourse with loud but illogical arguments. They deceive because we allow them to deceive.

---

[55] Clinton Cash: The Untold Story of How and Why Foreign Governments and Businesses Helped Make Bill and Hillary Rich Ch. 10(Harper Collins. Kindle Edition)

How Can We Succeed?
1. Frame the argument honestly.
2. Confront non sequiturs.
3. Expect and prepare to be attacked.
4. Don't participate in dismissive attitudes.
5. Finally, know what you believe and why you believe it.

Frame the Argument Honestly
Those who argue against free markets deceive by framing the argument dishonestly. The argument is not between "homeless families dying of hunger if taxes aren't raised." Socialists have historically twisted the truth, and we should not allow them to frame the discussion in simplistic and stupid arguments.

Confront Non Sequiturs
Non Sequitur comes from the Latin meaning *"it does not follow."* Confusion enters an argument when a person makes one or two points and then comes to a conclusion that has little to do with what they just said. You will hear many people say things like, "Corporations make too much money" or "One out of four corporations don't pay taxes." Then they conclude, "Corporations are evil," or "Corporations should not have the same rights as an individual Americans."

There is no way that one can argue against 4 statements that are all unrelated. If you dissect what a non-conservative says when arguing, you will find little reasoning; just statements that sound factual but are, mostly half-truths or lies.

For example, Berny Sanders (Socialist Democratic Presidential Candidate) said the statement above, "One in four corporations doesn't pay any taxes."[56] This is a half-truth that deceives. Here is why.

Since 2009 my wife and I have had an "S" Corporation in the State of California. "S" Corporations are Small Corporations that are owned by individuals or couples. These "S" Corp's profits flow through to the

---

[56] http://www.brainyquote.com/quotes/quotes/b/berniesand505489.html

individual's tax returns and the person pays individual taxes upon all corporate profits; every last cent.

It is true our "S" Corp has never paid taxes as a corporation. BUT taxes were paid on all profits of the corporation. Does Berny know he is deceiving? Does he care? A half-truth followed by a conclusion that *does not follow* should be called out and clarified.

Expect To Be Attacked

Let us not be stopped because of fear. Many of us stand up and are called bigots because we feel same-sex sexual behavior is a sin. We are accused of being in favor of "backroom abortions" because we are against abortion on demand. The same happens to those who stand up for freedom in the markets of the world. While trying to have a debate about government health care, Florida Representative Alan Grayson attacked all Republicans by accusing them of wanting people who are sick to, "Die quickly."[57]

Name calling, boycotts and other bullying actions will be used to stop men who fight for free markets. Those who are against freedom do not want the truth to be voiced. Don't let them shout you down.

Dismissive Attitudes toward Capitalism

To self-rule we must have debates about controversial issues. We believe our positions are morally superior, but we must stand and voice why we believe these views are right and our opponient's views are wrong.

Don't immediately dismiss another's argument; be respectful and be ready to NOT win your opponent over to your side. But don't let your opponent dismiss your point of view. This is done by his laughter, or non-responses to your points. Debate that builds a GOOD Democracy should have intelligent responses. Maybe that is why so many people no longer call for a debate, only a conversation. We must have more than a conversation. We must be respected in our opposing opinions.

---

[57] http://www.motherjones.com/politics/2010/01/best-quotes-alan-grayson

Is God A Capitalist?

Know What You Believe and Why You Believe It

With Google and the internet, most statistics can be researched in one minute. Don't believe what the government says. Become a healthy skeptic of the "facts" and discern hidden agendas. As a follower of God, be a sheep. But when it comes to men in power be wise and discerning.

The above statements from Berny Sanders are a perfect example. A quick Google search will uncover how the stats about corporations paying taxes have been twisted. This book and others by Thomas Sowell, Dennis Prager and Dinesh D'Souza can provide truth that will shine light upon the many lies now spoken with such conviction from the anti-capitalist crowd.

We don't have to be disrespectful in our confrontation. But we should no longer be silent. As we watch our local, county, state and federal governments become more oppressive, we should STAND and FIGHT.

Finally, talk to your kids about morals and money. Find the brainwashing that is probably already happening in your child's good Christian schools. Because these subjects are rarely discussed, you kids are probably already on their way to indoctrination. The principles of Marxism are taught as fact in many elementary and middle schools; even Christian Schools.

Send this book to your Pastor, Christian School Principle, Small Group Leader or Deacon and ask them about their positions on these subjects. If they answer you with unclear, uneducated ideas, consider finding another group of Christians to associate with. Or be a respectful messenger of facts and begin to confront your leaders when you hear Marx quoted from the platform.

Pray, Speak, Study and Vote.

11

What the Bible Says About Wealth
Faithful Servants Are Good Stewards

Wealth is a big subject and this is a little chapter. This chapter is included to bring clarity about the scriptural statements about riches. If we distort the Bible's messages about money, we can misunderstand God's preference in financial systems.

If a man has good health, good friends and a loving family, he is a wealthy man indeed. But when we talk about having material wealth, it does not have to be an either-or proposal. Life has many trade-offs and no one can have it all. But when it comes to wealth, both physical wealth and relationship wealth are both an expression of God's blessings, if we keep our priorities right.

Man's Ultimate Goal
Thus says the Lord, "Let not a wise man boast of his wisdom, and let not the mighty man boast of his might, let not a rich man boast of his riches; but let him who boasts boast of this, that he understands and knows Me, that I am the Lord who exercises lovingkindness, justice and righteousness on earth; for I delight in these things," declares the Lord. *Jeremiah 9:23-24 NASB*

I had been a pastor for about 10 years, when I felt the Holy Spirit convict me of not ministering to rich people. It was true. I had taken James 2:1-3's admonition about not being partial to the rich to the opposite extreme. I happily ministered to the poor and the middle class, but avoided those who appeared rich.

God opened my heart to not be intimidated by those who are viewed as rich and minister to them as I would any other man. Obviously they needed God's love as much as other men do. So what had made me ignore rich men? It was a misreading of the story of Jesus' encounter with The Rich Young Ruler.

Is God A Capitalist?

The Saddest Story of the New Testament

As He (*Jesus*) was setting out on a journey, a man ran up to Him and knelt before Him, and asked Him, "Good Teacher, what shall I do to inherit eternal life?" And Jesus said to him, "Why do you call Me good? No one is good except God alone.

You know the commandments, 'Do not murder, Do not commit adultery, Do not steal, Do not bear false witness, Do not defraud, Honor your father and mother.'" And he said to Him, "Teacher, I have kept all these things from my youth up." Looking at him, Jesus felt a love for him.... *Mark 10:17-21a NASB*

This young man was full of energy and excited to see Jesus. Jesus' first response wasn't a rebuke but a question to draw the young man out. Remember, the people around Jesus had many opinions about Him. Jesus was drawing the young man into a conversation about Himself. And as the young man responded, Jesus looked at him and felt a great love for him. And then something very unique happened. Jesus gave him a personal invitation to become one of his disciples.

Looking at him, Jesus felt a love for him and said to him, "One thing you lack: go and sell all you possess and give to the poor, and you will have treasure in heaven; and come, follow Me."

But at these words he was saddened, and he went away grieving, for he was one who owned much property. And Jesus, looking around, said to His disciples, "How hard it will be for those who are wealthy to enter the kingdom of God!" *Mark 10:21-23 NASB*

After becoming one of the few in the Bible account, personally invited to become one of Jesus' disciples, the rich young man declined the invitation. He could not see himself selling everything he had. But something else was happening behind the scenes. Jesus' comment about rich men entering the Kingdom of God had perplexed his disciples.

The disciples were amazed at His words. But Jesus answered again and said to them, "Children, how hard it is to enter the kingdom of God! It is easier for a camel to go through the eye of a needle than for a rich man to enter the kingdom of God."

They were even more astonished and said to Him, "Then who can be saved?" Looking at them, Jesus said, "With people it is impossible, but not with God; for all things are possible with God." *Mark 10:24-27 NASB*

The Snare of Riches

If we have food and covering, with these we shall be content. But those who want to get rich fall into temptation and a snare and many foolish and harmful desires which plunge men into ruin and destruction.

For the love of money is a root of all sorts of evil, and some by longing for it have wandered away from the faith and pierced themselves with many griefs. *I Timothy 6:8-10 NASB*

So Jesus stated that rich people have a hard time getting into the kingdom of God and Paul's exhortation is that we should avoid the "love of money." Well that settles it. Christians are destined to be poor; Right? But wait, read the rest of the story. (Also Ma. 19 & Lu. 18) Peter, a small businessman who left his business continued:

Peter began to say to Him, "Behold, we have left everything and followed You." [*Matthew inserts here in 19:27*] "what then will there be for us?")

Jesus said, "Truly I say to you, there is no one who has left house or brothers or sisters or mother or father or children or farms, for My sake and for the gospel's sake, but that **he will receive a hundred times as much now in the present age,** houses and brothers and sisters and mothers and children and farms, along with persecutions; and in the age to come, eternal life. But many who are first will be last, and the last, first." *Mark 10:28-31 NASB emphasis added*

Jesus concludes His statements about how hard it is for the rich to get into the kingdom with the pronouncement that those who DO follow him will receive more in this age than they gave up. Houses and farms are real property plus relationships. Some Christians have only believed in the persecutions part of this promise.

Two Truths in Tension

1. It is hard for rich people to be saved. This is easy to understand. If your trust is in your assets, there is no reason to seek salvation.
2. Everyone who enters the Kingdom of God has a promise of present day riches and eternal rewards.

Well Done Good and Faithful Servant

The Bible does not universally condemn the rich or exalt the poor. The Bible's emphasis is on our stewardship of that which we have. We will all give account of how we used our money, time, energy, skills, and talents. Stewardship is the issue.

"For it *(the Kingdom of God)* is just like a man about to go on a journey, who called his own slaves and entrusted his possessions to them. To one he gave five talents, to another, two, and to another, one, each according to his own ability; and he went on his journey.

Immediately the one who had received the five talents went and traded with them, and gained five more talents. In the same manner the one who had received the two talents gained two more. But he who received the one talent went away, and dug a hole in the ground and hid his master's money.

"Now after a long time the master of those slaves came and settled accounts with them. The one who had received the five talents came up and brought five more talents, saying, 'Master, you entrusted five talents to me. See, I have gained five more talents.' His master said to him, 'Well done, good and faithful slave. You were faithful with a few things, I will put you in charge of many things; enter into the joy of your master.'

"Also the one who had received the two talents came up and said, 'Master, you entrusted two talents to me. See, I have gained two more talents.' His master said to him, 'Well done, good and faithful slave. You were faithful with a few things, I will put you in charge of many things; enter into the joy of your master...' *Matthew 25:14-23 NASB*

When reviewing your personal faithfulness, it is easy to review your stewardship of physical assets. Assets are measurable and can be easily counted. Your percentage of alms given to the poor is easily calculated. Our love for God and others is much harder to measure. Jesus addressed this problem of human beings accurately reviewing how they are doing in the heart areas of faithfulness. After telling a story about the stewardship of money, Jesus said:

"He who is faithful in a very little thing is faithful also in much; and he who is unrighteous in a very little thing is unrighteous also in much. Therefore if you have not been faithful in the use of unrighteous wealth, who will entrust the true riches to you?

And if you have not been faithful in the use of that which is another's, who will give you that which is your own? No servant can serve two masters; for either he will hate the one and love the other, or else he will be devoted to one and despise the other. You cannot serve God and wealth." *Luke 16:10-13 NASB*

We are not supposed to love money or serve riches, but we are to be faithful managers of the assets that God has given us. This same balanced approach to stewardship is echoed by Paul in his exhortations to the Christians in Corinth.

Each of you should give as you have decided in your heart to give. You should not be sad when you give, and you should not give because you feel forced to give. God loves the person who gives happily. And **God can give you more blessings than you need**. Then you will always have plenty of everything—enough to give to every good work. It is written in the Scriptures:

"He gives freely to the poor.
The things he does are right and will continue forever."

God is the One who gives seed to the farmer and bread for food. He will give you all the seed you need and make it grow so there will be a great harvest from your goodness. **He will make you rich in every way** so that you can always give freely. And your giving through us will cause many to give thanks to God. *II Corinthians 9:7-11 NCV emphasis added*

This passage again emphasizes God's intention to have rich children. We may enter into the Kingdom of God poor, but if we are good stewards and have a righteous and cautious attitude toward money, we will not stay poor.

The goal of the Christian is not to get rich so he can retire at thirty. We all have eternal purposes in our stewardship. We work with a motivation deeper than getting rich. We can take pleasure in our accomplishments because we are working for a higher purpose.

The sleep of the working man is pleasant, whether he eats little or much; but the full stomach of the rich man does not allow him to sleep. *Ecclesiastes 5:12 NASB*

The Warnings About Riches

There are two types of warnings to the Rich scattered throughout the scriptures. One type is directed to the ruling class and is predominately a warning about the misuse of power. The other type is the warnings about money directed toward everyone, whether poor or rich. It is these warnings to the non-rich that reveals God's heart for men to live with more than they need; God's desire for His children to create wealth.

Jesus' warning to the rich and poor is in Mark 4:19, *but the worries of the world, and the deceitfulness of riches, and the desires for other things enter in and choke the word, and it becomes unfruitful.* Everyone has to struggle with these three things that bring unfruitfulness. Ironically, the poor are many times more deceived by riches. The State Lotteries would not exist, if the non-rich were not deceived by riches.

Warnings about Trusting in Riches
He who trusts in his riches will fall,
But the righteous will flourish like the green leaf.
Proverbs 11:28 NASB
[Ps 49, Ps 52:6-8, Ps 62:10; I Tim. 6: 6, 17; Isaiah 31:1]

The Futility of Riches
Riches do not profit in the day of wrath,
But righteousness delivers from death.
Proverbs 11:4 NASB
[Ps 39:6, Pr 27:24, Ec. 4:8, 5:10, 6:2; Luke 12:21, James 1:10-11; 5:1-3]

Attaining Riches by Unrighteousness
A faithful man will abound with blessings,
But he who makes haste to be rich will not go unpunished.
Proverbs 28:20 NASB
[Pr 1:18-19, 10:2, 11:16; Ma. 16:26, Luke 16:19-26, Ha 2:6]

Job's Restoration - Chapter 42
The Lord restored the fortunes of Job when he prayed for his friends, and the Lord increased all that Job had twofold. Then all his brothers and all his sisters and all who had known him before came to him, and they ate bread with him in his house; and they consoled him and comforted him for all the adversities that the Lord had brought on him. And each one gave him one piece of money, and each a ring of gold.

The Lord blessed the latter days of Job more than his beginning; and he had 14,000 sheep and 6,000 camels and 1,000 yoke of oxen and 1,000 female donkeys. He had seven sons and three daughters. He named the first Jemimah, and the second Keziah, and the third Keren-happuch. In all the land no women were found so fair as Job's daughters; and their father gave them inheritance among their brothers.

After this, Job lived 140 years, and saw his sons and his grandsons, four generations. And Job died, an old man and full of days. *Job 42:10-17 NASB*

Abraham & Lot

Now Abram was very rich in livestock, in silver and in gold. He went on his journeys from the Negev as far as Bethel, to the place where his tent had been at the beginning, between Bethel and Ai… Now Lot, who went with Abram, also had flocks and herds and tents. And the land could not sustain them while dwelling together, for their possessions were so great that they were not able to remain together. *Genesis 13:2-3, 5-6 NASB*

Isaac

Now Isaac sowed in that land and reaped in the same year a hundredfold. And the Lord blessed him, and the man became rich, and continued to grow richer until he became very wealthy; for he had possessions of flocks and herds and a great household, so that the Philistines envied him. *Genesis 26:12-14 NASB*

Paul the Apostle

I know how to get along with humble means, and I also know how to live in prosperity; in any and every circumstance I have learned the secret of being filled and going hungry, both of having abundance and suffering need. **I can do all things through Him who strengthens me**. *Philippians 4:12-13 NASB emphasis added*

Assorted Promises about Wealth

Psalms 112:1-3 - Promises of wealth to the Christian
Proverbs 3:16; Proverbs 8:18 - Wisdom brings wealth
Proverbs 22:4 - The reward of humility is riches
Ecclesiastes 5:19 - God wants us to be blessed by our riches
Isaiah 61-5-7 - Promised riches and a double portion
Luke 16:11 - Faithfulness with money brings a spiritual blessing

12

Bible Charity
God's Safety Net

When God established the small limited government of the Times of the Judges, he had the ability to establish any number of safety nets for those who were truly poor.

So let us look at the methods and practical applications of the Bible in dealing with the poor. When approaching the subject of helping the poor, I will divide poverty into three different types.

Three Types of Poverty
1. Long term mistakes or misfortune producing generational poverty
2. Short term need from life circumstances
3. The Dependent – Widows and Orphans

Most Christians understand that it is God's desire for them to give to the poor. Historically Christians have voluntarily tried to rescue and feed those in poverty. God's goal when He instituted His limited government in the Times of the Judges was that there would be none who were poor in Israel.

> … there will be no poor among you, since the Lord will surely bless you in the land which the Lord your God is giving you as an inheritance to possess, if only you listen obediently to the voice of the Lord your God, to observe carefully all this commandment which I am commanding you today. *Deut. 15:4-5 NASB*

Unfortunately the "IF" of verse 5 was the only way the country could experience this 00% poverty rate. Jesus told us we would not win the Secular War on Poverty 2000 years ago.

"For you always have the poor with you…" *Matthew 26:11a NASB*

As Bible believing Christians, we accept the fact that men are sinful and sinful activity will bring men to poverty; spiritual poverty, emotional poverty, mental poverty and physical poverty. God being a fair and just God will allow men to have what they work for, even if this means they suffer loss. His justice is manifest by not intervening in unrighteous men's affairs. When he does intervene and help men, who do not deserve help, we call this action God's mercy.

Confused Language – Confused Approach

21st Century language has been corrupted by political activists. We now use words in their opposite meaning. When we address helping the poor we talk about Social Justice. As Chapter 4 detailed, Social Justice is not justice at all. Social Justice is Social Mercy. What is mistakenly called Social Justice is really someone intervening and stopping men from getting what they deserve.

For example, when a man is an alcoholic and loses his job because of his inability to be at work, he may become homeless. When the church tries to help him with housing, food, or clothing, it is charity. These are mercy gifts. The man deserves to get exactly what his actions have brought upon him, but the generous and kindhearted in the church reach out to the hurting to help. It is not the man's RIGHT to be helped. It is our love and mercy for him that tries to rescue him.

As Christians we are to have compassion for the poor, including the poor who deserve to be poor. But we are also to be wise in how we try to help. As a pastor, I counseled a young man named Brian.

> Brian was a young father of three. He had struggled with recreational drug use and the financial problems that accompany it. He attended our church regularly and was open about his problem. He had struggled with getting his finances in order, as he periodically slipped back into drug and alcohol use.

> One of his problems was that he didn't have a car and in Southern California, it is almost impossible to work without some type of transportation. We prayed and Brian found an old car and bought it.

Within two months, Brian had disappeared and lost his job. The car had given him the ability to get a job. But the money from the job and the mobility of the having a car had given him the freedom to buy drugs. He quickly fell back into poverty.

Was Brian's problem poverty or sinful choices? The government's attempt to help Brian not "be poor" failed each time the cold bureaucracy responded to his requests for help. Once his children grew up and left home, he also left his wife and I have not seen him since. How sad. His children still talk to me about him. They love him, but never see him.

Our challenge as Christians is how to use God's wisdom to create a secular safety net that rescues people and does not help them maintain a destructive lifestyle that will ultimately destroy them, and hurt their family.

The Old and New Testament has commands, insights and exhortations that can guide us as we seek justice and give appropriate mercy.

7 Insights on Bible Charity

I. Charity Should Be Voluntary
I Corinthians 9:7 gives direct orders to only give donations to help the poor voluntarily. Old Testament giving was also voluntary.

II. Short Term Help Should Require Work
The story of Ruth is a story of short term help to someone experiencing life tragedies. God told the business people in the rural economy of the day; farmer businessmen to not harvest the corners of their fields. (*Leviticus 19:9-10*) This type of charity requires some work and does not take away the dignity of the receiver. If laziness was the main reason that a person was poor, they would stay hungry because they would miss the gleaning times. Then their hunger may be a motivator to change the real problem; their life habits.

III. Long Term Help for Dependent Individuals

As Apostle Paul would say, "… assist those who are widows indeed." *(I Timothy 5:16 NASB)* A society has to decide what to do with the truly dependent people among them. The blind, extremely disabled and older widows are easily identified. The question is what process should be used to help these individuals. When I was in China in 1993, a mentally handicapped boy came and sat with us on a train. At that time China had few mentally disabled children. They simply disappeared and we wondered how this boy had survived.

IV. Personal & Local Charity

The story of Ruth reveals another principle of Israel's systematic safety net. The close relatives were supposed to help the destitute of their family. In Ruth's story Boaz rescues her, because he is a relative.

Paul also uses this approach when the 1st Century Church was administrating long term help to the widows in the church.

> But if anyone does not provide for his own, and especially for those of his household, he has denied the faith and is worse than an unbeliever.

> A widow is to be put on the list *(for church support)* only if she is not less than sixty years old, having been the wife of one man, having a reputation for good works… But refuse to put younger widows on the list… Therefore, I want younger widows to get married, bear children, keep house… I Timothy 5:8-10a, 11a, 14a

Although aid to the elderly may give them independence, it can also isolate them from their relatives. That is why Paul starts with the exhortation that, if you are a believer you should personally take care of your relatives. Intergenerational connections bring stability to families and societies. Isolating granny in a government funded nursing home robs the next generation of granny's insights, love and wisdom. There may be times that medical conditions require long term care, but this should be the last resort.

In Ruth's story, it is obvious by Boaz' consulting the elders (our equivalent of local government) and also by Paul's requirements for long term care that charity should be overseen by local, personal and compassionate people who know the people involved.

V. The Limited Parameters of Charity

Continuing with the theme set by Paul, when addressing long term care for the elderly, the amount of help should also be limited. Gleaning fields and vineyards gave the receiver of the charity, the dignity of working to get their own meal. It also restricted how much food could be received, since the amount to glean was limited.

Most knew the owner of the field. Everyone would know the miserly and the generous. The system had systematic accountability for the giver and the receiver, even in the voluntary obedience to the Law. The landowner could be thanked or resented depending upon the businessman's actions.

> For we have brought nothing into the world, so we cannot take anything out of it either. If we have food and covering, with these we shall be content *I Timothy 6:7-8 NASB*

Paul set his apostolic team's minimum requirements to food and covering in the above scripture. Jesus also when talking about how God loves His children and is concerned that their needs are met stated:

> Do not worry then, saying, 'What will we eat?' or 'What will we drink?' or 'What will we wear for clothing?' For the Gentiles eagerly seek all these things; for your heavenly Father knows that you need all these things. But seek first His kingdom and His righteousness, and all these things will be added to you. *Matthew 6:31-33 NASB*

This passage has a deeper meaning than defining what we need, but it does detail God's heart of understanding to all of us humans who need food, water and clothing. Our systematic help to the poor should be limited to the basics.

Successful Failure

The attempts of our present system, to raise people out of poverty by charity have succeeded. As I described in Chapter 5, subheading *The Poor Get Poorer*, the poor in America now spend as much money as the lower middle class, because of government charity.

The Charity has succeeded and failed because it has made the poor permanently dependent upon help. The success has trapped people in poverty. I have been told by my employees that they would like to work more. But if they worked more hours, they would lose their benefits. They could make $250 more a month, but would lose $500 of government benefits. Our goal should be to help until it is not needed; not creating a permanent underclass forever dependent upon long term support.

VI. Will Work for Food

Poverty is a great motivator. I taught my children the value of their work, by paying them for tasks. I balanced family chores (no pay), gifts (not earned) and projects that were only rewarded, once the work was completed. I am proud that I taught them a work ethic. They understand that work is not scary and if they persevere they will be rewarded.

> For even when we were with you, we used to give you this order: if anyone is **not willing to work, then he is not to eat**, either. For we hear that some among you are leading an undisciplined life, doing no work at all, but acting like busybodies. Now such persons we command and exhort in the Lord Jesus Christ to **work** in quiet fashion and **eat their own** bread. *II Thessalonians 3:10-12 NASB emphasis added*

Long term charity is not to be given to those who are not willing to work. We should not let idleness; laziness or a lack of direction rob a person of their motivation to work. Long term charity always creates more problems than it solves, when disconnected from work. If we love the poor, work should be encouraged and idleness discouraged.

VII. The Year of Jubilee

Every 49th year Israel was commanded to celebrate the Year of Jubilee and return specific farmlands back to the family that had inherited it initially. Because of the prohibition of charging interest to fellow Israelites, and the forgiveness of debt every seven years, long term debt was not a systematic problem. Generational poverty experienced a reset every seven years and property ownership was reestablished every 49 years.[58]

The Year of Jubilee satisfied God's promise to Abraham that Abraham's Seed would always be owners of the Land of Israel. It also accomplished a charitable reset for the children of one generation that had not participated in the behavior of the former generation. Bad stewardship from sinful or incompetent behavior can take away the next generation's inheritance. Over consumption of one generation can lock the next into poverty that was not of their making.

We cannot systematically do a "property reset" like the Year of Jubilee. But we could start to speak loudly about how one generation can rob the next generation. It is ironic that socialistic idealists are younger. They do not understand they are voting for policies and programs that are robbing them of their inheritance.

All free markets have resets when they are tampered with by those who would game the system. These systematic resets are viewed as bad, when they are actually similar to the Year of Jubilee. When government or rich men distort the markets, the markets reset. The more moral behavior by government and investors, the less resets happen.

The Robin Hood Method
IS NOT Christian Charity

Throughout history there have always been groups of people who decided that they should take other people's property. They have been organized in many forms. By force or the threat of violence, they have taken what they have not worked for.

---

[58] Leviticus 25:10; Deuteronomy 15:1; Leviticus 25:36

African warlords, bands of robbers, kings and queens of kingdoms, dictators of nations; every group had their own reasons for taking what was not theirs. Some convinced themselves that they had a right to it. Others do not care who has the right to what you have earned, but believe that the strong should be rewarded for their strength. Throughout history this principle of *"To the victor goes the spoils,"* has guided immoral men. A shining exception, to this rule was Bible based communities.

As Christians historically, we have stood against the tyranny of dictators and the anarchy of war lords. But we have not yet seen our mission; to stand against the biggest robber barons of the last century. The 20th Century birthed a new way to take people's property. Instead of bullies or kings with armies taking our property and keeping it for themselves, governments take it. They then give a percentage back to those who voted them into power.

This tyranny of the voter has confused many Christians and deceived them into thinking that God wanted the poor taken care of, through the present unjust system. A democracy finds its legitimacy through the protection of the individual from the tyranny of the majority.

Today, the United States is doing an adequate job of protecting the individual from injustice in court proceedings; protection of minorities from discrimination; protecting individual freedom of sexual behavior; and other freedoms that the courts and activists have fought to protect.

Today, the United States is doing a very poor job in protecting the individual from the tyranny of the majority, when it comes to wealth redistribution and freedom to practice religion in the public square.

Deceived Christians continue to vote for politicians that do not protect the individual from the tyranny of the majority. Politicians no longer hide behind high sounding phrases. They now just say, "Elect me and I will take money from your rich neighbors and give it to you." They leave out the fact that the gigantic bureaucracy they will create, to do this will take a large cut of the money, before redistribution.

People who vote for the Robin Hood politicians are voting for tyranny of the majority. It will only be a short time that this tyranny will attack ALL individual freedom.

The Robin Hood Politician's Excuses

The Robin Hood's politicians need to come up with excuses of why it is OK to take from one man and give to another. Here are a few excuses you may have heard.

1. A country as rich as the United States should not neglect helping those in need.

This is a true statement. But this question is usually framed as either you do it my way or it won't be done at all. Most Americans and most Christians want to help the poor. But doing it through large federal bureaucracies is counterproductive.

2. We have enough money, because we are a rich nation.

This is only a temporary truth, told by men and women who continually tell us that they do not have enough money, to do the things they want to do.

Ironically, these same people who always tell us that we have enough money, to do whatever they want to do also tell us that;
> People who eat too much cost the public too much money;
> People who smoke cost the public too much money;
> People who drink too much cost the public too much money.

Every socialist government has run out of money, to do what they want to do, sooner or later. After raising taxes, borrowing money and finally just printing money, the money finally runs out.

3. It is not moral for men to be richer than everyone else.

Democratic candidate for President, Bernie Sanders was quoted in Chapter 10, saying it was immoral to have wealth in only a few people's hands. As Christians we should ask Bernie where he gets his moral code. We do not decide what is moral. God does. A Socialist's morality is rooted in atheists' doctrines. Who's morality will you follow; Berny and Marx's or God's?

4. Rich men do not deserve to keep their property.

This is an irrational statement. Since our laws stop men from illegally acquiring wealth, legally acquired wealth is owned by the owner, period.

How Long Term Charity Corrupts Men's Hearts

1. It encourages laziness and idleness.
2. It produces a lack of healthy ambition.
3. It creates a distorted view of justice.
4. It produces a sense of entitlement that breeds covetousness.
5. It encourages a self-centered focus upon personal needs.
6. It creates a closed heart toward other's needs.
7. It births a twisted thinking of what is really important.
8. It robs the person of the dignity of taking care of their family.

What Should We Do?

1. Start by voting the Robin Hood politicians out of office, no matter what they call themselves.
2. Change our Christian culture to use restraint when asking the government to do anything.
3. Allow faith based organizations to receive grants to do specific rescue operations on a local level.
4. Replace all federal programs that try to help the poor and create processes for local governments to provide "last resort" services in their own communities.
5. Change our thinking from government charity to personal charity.
6. All Safety Net programs should be limited, monitored and only available to those who are willing to work.
7. Financial responsibility should be held up as the IDEAL. Needing more than short term help should be frowned on by everyone, unless there is a long-term disability.
8. Churches should be taught and encouraged to elevate charity as important as their building programs and other missions.
9. Pastors should discern deceptions about government charity.

A Final Word

As I write this, we in the United States are having an election that has a clear distinction, between those who believe in big government and those who do not. The next election is very, very important for the direction of our country. We are already, Biblically going the wrong direction. But it is not just who is President that is our problem.

Our real problem is Christian ignorance and Christian deception. Jimmy Carter was a born again Christian. Yet Jimmy Carter made no decisions that would not have been made by an anti-church, anti-religion, anti-capitalist atheist.

We need to find a president that has correct values. But even more, we need to stand up and fight for free markets, free enterprise and a financially moral society. If we lose our Christian values, we will have a society that is no longer what our founding fathers envisioned.

Finally, we should realize that America is not a theocracy and that being too dogmatic or too fundamental in our expectations of political outcomes can be an unrighteous position. We should be a PART, an important part, of the public discourse. But IF we cannot win a debate, then we should lose graciously and keep debating.

Some think that because we are working for God's values, we should never "settle." I think that we should have the wisdom to know when to compromise and when to fight. And then CLEARLY define why we oppose those whom we disagree with. Taking a position that never compromises may be fundamentally correct, while we lose the war. We should review and then fight for many moral political positions; but only fight to the death for a few that we feel are non-negotiable.

Let us be the wisest ones in public debate.

Let us shine in the public places for righteousness and freedom.

Appendix I

An Eye for an Eye
The Doctrine of Justice

Everyone wants to be treated justly. Our country's court system is called the Justice System because we all want justice. We all want our neighbors, children and friends to be treated fairly and obtain justice when they are wronged. God wants justice too.

> "You have heard that it was said, 'An eye for an eye, and a tooth for a tooth.' But I say to you, do not resist an evil person; but whoever slaps you on your right cheek, turn the other to him also. If anyone wants to sue you and take your shirt, let him have your coat also. Whoever forces you to go one mile, go with him two. Give to him who asks of you, and do not turn away from him who wants to borrow from you. *Matthew 5:38-42 NASB*

The Law
> Thus you shall not show pity: life for life, eye for eye, tooth for tooth, hand for hand, foot for foot. *Deuteronomy 19:21 NASB*

Justice under the Law of Moses was appropriate. Justice was required to be blind to the offender and victim. Justice's punishment fit the crime. Those listening to Jesus that day knew His frame of reference. They knew the "Eye for an Eye" verse describing the Justice of God. Jesus started His discourse with the following.

> "Do not think that I came to abolish the Law or the Prophets; I did not come to abolish but to fulfill. For truly I say to you, until heaven and earth pass away, not the smallest letter or stroke shall pass from the Law until all is accomplished. *Matthew 5:17-18 NASB*

Jesus was not changing the practice of seeking justice in the public courts. Nor would we want to see our courts, distort Justice.

Appendix I

Is It Right to Seek Justice for Another?

Thus says the Lord, "Do justice and righteousness, and deliver the one who has been robbed from the power of his oppressor. Also do not mistreat or do violence to the stranger, the orphan, or the widow; and do not shed innocent blood in this place. *Jeremiah 22:3 (also Isaiah 1:17 & 16:5; Proverbs 29:26)*

What Was Jesus Saying?

Jesus' exhortation was to individuals; specifically having one on one encounters. In personal confrontations, you should NOT try to seek justice for YOURSELF. By taking this position that you, personally will not insist on your right to have justice, you will position yourself as the one in the conflict that may bring resolution. Jesus is saying that *turning the other cheek* is being prepared to be the peacemaker, before a confrontation. If you are interested in winning the person "slapping" you, you can intentionally overlook the obvious wrong.

If you are personally bullied into doing something that you would not normally do, relax and go "The Extra Mile." By doing this, not out of fear, laziness or passivity; but out of a sense of mission, you have a better chance on winning the bully.

Approaching minor personal conflicts, with the mission to win the other person also saves us from the disappointments of life. So many times we do not find true or full justice in this life. Life is full of injustices that are never resolved. When we give up our right to be seen as the victim; the one who needs retribution; we free ourselves from future bitterness. We stand relaxed as a witness of Jesus' love for others. This mental position of "Not insisting on our rights," allows us to get out of God's way and allows Him to work for full justice.

God can help us have grace and see clearly the act; not minimizing, distorting or pretending that what was done was OK. Seeing clearly, we can still NOT seek our rights to justice. We can be prepared to NOT be the victim, with God's help. Jesus was talking about changing our perspective, not the facts of whether something was right or wrong.

Appendix I

What Jesus Did NOT Say

1. Jesus did NOT say that governments should not seek justice at all times. Governments cannot "turn other people's cheeks."
2. Jesus did NOT say that you should stand by idly and allow evil to steal, kill or destroy without resisting it.
3. Jesus did NOT say that justice (an eye for an eye) is not good.
4. Jesus did NOT say that His kingdom would not be a kingdom of justice.
5. Jesus did NOT say to turn other people's cheeks for them. If someone steals from your family, you should seek justice for your children and your wife, and still find a place of peace, personally.
6. Jesus did NOT say that you are to avoid helping the courts or others when they seek justice in your case, or other's cases.
7. Jesus did NOT say that He was changing the definition of small insults and bullying and they were no longer considered wrong behavior.

Because Jesus was talking to those under the Law of Moses, He could talk with confidence that the principle of Justice would not be distorted. The listeners were fully aware of the importance of Justice. It is only after we see the importance and nature of justice that we can live out the *turn the other cheek* dynamic, correctly.

Definition of Justice

Justice is a person getting exactly what he deserves. Perfect justice is a person getting exactly what he deserves, all the time, in every circumstance.

Perfect justice is blind; to who the person; his status in life; how rich he is or how poor he is. It may take into account the circumstances and intentions of each act, to find a perfectly appropriate punishment. If a man steals a loaf of bread to save his family from starving, he should be treated differently from a person who stole the same loaf of bread out of resentment toward the rich shop owner.

Perfect justice must be left to God, since only He can evaluate everything. So only after death and in eternity will we see perfect justice. But the fact that we will never fully succeed in our goal of

Appendix I

perfect justice does not stop God from asking us to seek justice and act appropriately. We are His children and we represent His attitudes toward Justice on the Earth.

The Definition of Mercy

Mercy is a person NOT getting what he deserves. We all want mercy for ourselves and our loved ones. Although our heart hates to see injustice; someone else getting away with bad actions; when it comes to ourselves and our loved ones; we hope for mercy.

As we understand that God demands justice, we who want mercy run into the saving grace of Jesus' sacrifice. Unless we really, really see eternal JUSTICE as a quality of a good God, we will never fully appreciate the mercy we receive, through the sacrifice of the Passover lamb.

Financial Systems & Government Justice

In secular relationships between human beings, governments should be held to the standard of JUSTICE. Appropriate mercy can be a part of these secular judgments against wrong behavior. But the legal systems of our world that keep civilization from breaking down into chaos should never institute systematic injustice. One way government retains its authority is that those who submit to its authority view government as treating everyone impartially.

Christians have a unique place to witness in our world. We can model in our personal relationships loving behavior in which we give up our right to be right; our right to be the victim. And we can also vigorously fight for justice for everyone. May we all "win" the heart of that personal enemy at work that is treating us badly. May we also be known as those who seek justice for everyone else.

About the Author

GREGORY B GRINSTEAD was senior pastor of Palmdale Christian Fellowship, a church in Southern California for over 25 years.

Gregory and his wife Michelle have four adult children and are currently living in Southern California and Kansas City. They minister in churches throughout the United States.

Gregory is also the author of the following books.

The Hidden Promise
How to Honor Your Parents

God's Help for Parents with Adult Children
Hope and Healing for Extended Family Relationships

You can email the author at *Gregory.B.Grinstead@gmail.com*